REFLECTIONS
Volume II

After spending his early years in the tiny Kent village of Wouldham, near Rochester, the author now lives in nearby Chatham. Married, with two sons, he works in a laboratory and as a carer in his spare time.

He has injected his less poignant work with a sense of humour, and keeps verses short, and easy to read. He has reflected on his life and family, plus slightly exaggerated versions of mishaps encountered at work, entwined with observations of the disabled and their harrowing situations, in an enjoyable and enthusiastic style.

REFLECTIONS
Volume II

Jim Bell

REFLECTIONS
Volume II

Olympia Publishers
London

www.olympiapublishers.com
OLYMPIA PAPERBACK EDITION

A CIP catalogue record for this title is
available from the British Library.

ISBN: 978-1-905513-56-7

First Published in 2008

**Olympia Publishers
60 Cannon Street
London
EC4N 6NP**

Printed in Great Britain

Dedication

To my wife, Dolly,

Nick and Sarah,
Richard and Gemma
And my beautiful grandchildren,
Paige, Jenson, Molly and Charlie.

Acknowledgement

And, not forgetting Dean and Ian
Without whose help this book
Would be "hand written".

Thank you both.

Section 8

THROUGH
THE EYES OF A CHILD

HERE MISS

Mum stops outside the playground,
And straightens her five year old's tie;
Tucks his shirt-tail into his waist band,
Fighting tears, as she says, "Goodbye".

A tenuous step beyond the gate,
Lunch box in his hand;
Gigantic satchel on his back,
Transformed into a little man.

Teachers and helpers, with outstretched arms,
To show newcomers where to go;
A glance back over his shoulder,
Trying not to let his teardrops flow.

The first day at school is daunting,
He's given a peg that bears his name;
Somewhere to hang his satchel and coat,
And a brown folder, labelled the same.

Guided through every minute of the day,
Newcomers get lots of attention;
Making friends with other children,
Far too many to mention.

Added to the register, on teacher's desk,
Say, "Here, Miss", when she calls your name;
Life in school on the very first day,
Is anything but a game.

When the bell rings, it's time to go home,
Mum thinks he'll be filled with sorrow;
But he settled in class, and made new pals,
And can't wait to get back there tomorrow.

KITTED OUT

The letter from the local school
Said, "We're afraid it's already full,
So we can't put the name of your child down.
He'll have to go elsewhere,
There's lots of schools out there,
Though some are on the far side of the town."

There was one we went and viewed,
Whose facilities were quite crude;
Playgrounds of tarmac – not a single blade of grass.
Mothers congregate to meet,
As their children pour out on the street,
We were astounded at how fast vehicles shot past.

Another boasted of its pride,
And looked good from the outside;
Children all wore uniforms, from day one.
When we visited, we could tell,
The teachers responded well,
And assured us of our child's future curriculum.

We didn't need a lot of persuading,
As we broke into our savings;
We bought grey trousers, white shirts, and even school ties.
Sports shorts and coloured vest,
Then he put us to the test,
The most expensive football boots, he wanted to try.

Kitted out, with his lunchbox in his hand,
He found it difficult to stand,
For he'd got his bits all packed in a rucksack.
It had pencil, ruler, book and pen,
Eraser, notepad, to use when
He could get the bag off his back.

We must admit, he looked really smart,
For the day when he would start,
His blazer pocket had the emblem of the school.
He had pocket money in a purse,
A contact number for the school nurse,
Asked if he was nervous, he said, "Mum... I'm cool!"

He took everything in his stride,
And it filled our hearts with pride,
In uniform, we took a photo of him dressed.
We're now grateful to the local school,
For telling us that they were full,
When people see his picture in its frame they're quite impressed.

PRE-SCHOOL

Pre-school children, just starting out,
Learning what life is all about;
Cared for by minders, while mum does her job,
Costing the parents a good few bob.

Playing in a tray with water and sand,
Adults standing by to lend a hand;
Children giggling – anything goes,
Plastic aprons tied to protect their clothes.

The walls are covered with pictures they've made,
And tables have models that made the grade;
A record plays songs where all can join in,
As they learn the words, and are taught to sing.

Actions are learned to accompany the songs,
To clap and stamp and sing along;
Pictures are shown of animals and pets,
And the letters of the alphabet.

Allowed to run and wear themselves out,
With a time to be quiet, and a time to shout.
Teaching the child to do as they're told,
As their introduction to authority gradually unfolds.

Full of excitement, in a happy mood,
As mum returns to collect her brood;
Little fists clasping pictures they've done,
Souvenirs to take home, to mum.

SAY YOUR PRAYERS

Kneel down by your bedside,
Shut your little eyes;
Put your hands together,
Tilt your head up to the skies.

Say a prayer for mummy and daddy,
And poor people everywhere;
Don't forget your grandad,
Who's old, and got no hair.

Mustn't forget the pussycat,
The dog, and your pet rabbit;
It's good to say prayers regularly,
Once you get into the habit.

MY SATCHEL

My satchel's very heavy,
It's got all the bits I need;
To get me through my school work,
If I'm going to succeed.

I've got a ruler and a pencil,
A rubber and some ink;
There's bits I made with my chemistry set,
That will create quite a stink.

They say I need two set-squares,
And a compass... but to this day,
I don't know why I need it,
I've always found the way!

I've got a pen I had for Christmas,
And a box to hold my lunch,
My keys, so I can get in my house,
On a gigantic bunch.

There's a dictionary in my school bag,
And books in which to write;
I mustn't forget my P.E. kit,
When I get home tonight.

EARLY STARTER

How many times must I tell you?
Will you never learn?
The way that you're behaving,
Is a matter for concern.

You never, ever listen,
To anything I say;
If I've told you once, I've told you twice,
Forever, and a day.

I've shown you how to do things,
And offered good advice;
But do you ever take notice?
Maybe once or twice.

Now, listen to what I tell you,
While you're huddled in your bed;
We both work hard to clothe you,
Your belly's always fed.

Don't you think it's time to look around,
Think about getting a job?
You're spending too much time in bed,
You're turning into a slob.

I hope you're taking note of this,
Listening to what I say;
Plan now, for what's ahead of you,
Now you've had your first birthday!

SWINGING

Hold the ropes,
Kick your legs up high,
Lean back in the seat,
And swing to the sky.

After reaching the top,
You'll go into reverse,
Tuck your legs in,
Just like you rehearsed.

Your dad had shown you
How it's done,
As he sat on the swing,
Having fun.

He hadn't done this
Since he was a boy,
Now showing his skills
On his new toy.

You'll practice and practice
On that swing,
Until one day, you'll be
As good as him.

I know that for now,
You're a little lad,
But in a few years,
You'll be just like your dad.

THE TOY SHOP

We went to D&A Toy Shop,
With bits hanging from the ceiling;
Shelves stacked full of boxes,
Some you could only see by kneeling.

Baskets filled with dollies,
And all their different clothes;
All shapes and sizes of bicycles,
All lined up in rows.

Computer games, and jigsaw puzzles,
Piled up out of reach;
Chemistry sets, and musical instruments,
Toys to take to the beach.

Gifts for birthday parties,
Affordable for all the kids;
Some items cost a fortune,
In fact… several hundred quid.

It made my eyes pop open,
As we walked into the store;
I've never seen so many toys,
In one place before.

ODD SOCKS

He got his socks out of the drawer,
One was red, and one was blue;
He didn't blink an eyelid,
For in the drawer were quite a few.

When his mum saw what he'd done,
She said, "You've got odd socks".
He said he knew he hadn't,
Even though he had got lots.

He then assured his mother,
Who went along with his little game;
I know that they're not odd ones,
I've got another pair exactly the same.

BABIES

A little girl was playing, one day,
When she looked up at her mummy;
She looked worried, so she asked her,
"What's that in your tummy?"

"Why's it got so big and fat,
It never used to be;
Now it's round, just like a ball,
It's really puzzling me."

Her mum explained just what it was,
It could only happen to a lady;
The bulge that she was looking at,
Was a little baby.

She scratched her head and pondered,
And said, "So, now I know it's not a ball;
I'd like a baby in my tummy,
But I couldn't eat it all!"

TADPOLES

Once, I went down to the village pond,
To see how many tadpoles I could get;
I'd taken one of mum's old stockings,
And a stick to make a net.

For weeks, I'd had jam on my bread,
In fact, on everything;
I took the empty, washed out jar,
And round the neck I tied some string.

A packet of crisps in my pocket,
I remember I heard mum say,
As I rushed out of the kitchen door,
"Don't stay out all day."

When you're small, you never take notice,
Of anything that you're told;
You think it only applies to big kids,
Those more than six years old.

When I came home about teatime,
I said I hadn't gone very far;
As I proudly showed my catch off,
There was one tadpole in my jar.

THE FAIR

Do you remember going to the village fair,
With its music, and flashing lights?
You were allowed out past your bedtime,
For the fair looked better at night.

You went for a ride on the dodgem cars,
Seated next to your dad;
Mummy didn't want a go,
I think it made her tummy bad.

Then you were given a wooden stick,
On the end there was a hook;
If you caught a duck with a number on,
You could win a car, gun, or book.

They let you stand close at the coconut shy,
Amongst the bales of straw;
They gave you six balls to throw at the nuts,
You ran out, and had no more.

Dad said you didn't stand a chance,
So you haven't really lost face;
He said not many people win a nut,
They were probably glued in place.

NEW SHOES

I've got a pair of running shoes,
Mum bought them in the shop;
She made me try them on for size,
Told me to walk, then jump, then hop.

They cost a lot of money,
More money than I'd ever seen;
Mum took the cash out of her purse,
She could see I was very keen.

They were white, with great big rubber soles,
And colours down one side;
She said I had to try them on,
Cos my feet were very wide.

I was so proud of my brand new shoes,
That I wore them home that day;
Mum said we should put them in a bag,
But I told her, "No Way!"

I didn't want to take them off,
And couldn't wait to see the faces,
Of all the other kids at school,
As I beat them in all the races.

TEACHERS

When you went to school, on your very first day,
Mummy took you to the gate;
Children gathered in the playground,
Ready to meet their fate.

You'd heard stories of teachers giving the cane,
On the hand if you didn't behave;
The thought had frightened the life out of you,
It was something you didn't crave.

When you first entered the classroom,
Teacher told you to sit quiet as mice;
Then she ticked your names in the register,
And she seemed to be rather nice.

It shows you can't go by what people tell you,
To believe them, you'd be a fool;
On that first day you formed an opinion,
Now you can't wait to go to school.

JESUS

"Mummy… we've been learning about Jesus,
And he lives up in the sky;
He hasn't got a pair of wings,
So I guess he cannot fly."

"How does he stay upon the clouds?
Why doesn't he fall through?
How come he sees everything,
That we decide to do?"

"Teacher said that God's his father,
Who looks after everyone on Earth.
But I thought that Mary and Joseph,
Were there for the virgin birth."

"It's getting very confusing,
With all the stories I am told;
I really don't know what to believe,
And I'm still only five years old!"

THE ROCKPOOL

The rockpool looked inviting,
Though the stones were very wet;
He edged his way even nearer,
Got as close as he could get.

He lay down on his belly,
Put his fingers in the pool;
The water wasn't very warm,
In fact, it felt quite cool.

He pulled out clumps of seaweed,
Took off his shoes and socks;
Saw a little crab go scurrying,
And hide beneath the rocks.

Swivelling on his bottom,
He managed to dip a toe,
Into the little rockpool,
As far as it would go.

When his foot got really cold,
He wiped his toes and feet;
Put his shoes and socks back on,
The warmth was quite a treat.

It's a really lovely feeling,
When you do something out of the blue;
He dipped his feet in the pool today,
What do you intend to do?

AUNTIES VISIT

Auntie Mary came to stay,
I hadn't seen her for a while;
She hadn't got her teeth in,
When she gave a great big smile.

Her hair was always greasy,
And I knew she liked to smoke;
She was always coughing and spluttering,
The smell almost made me choke.

She picked me up in her great big hands,
And lifted me up high;
Then sat me down upon her lap,
Resting on her thigh.

She never wore any make-up,
And had blemishes on her skin;
Her nails were bitten unevenly,
A whisker grew from a mole on her chin.

The only reason I liked her staying,
And not paying mum any rent;
She always gave me some money,
Just before she went.

THE CIRCUS

One day, a caravan appeared
On the playing fields in the town;
They put up a great big notice board,
With a picture of a clown.

Then, some other men arrived,
And erected a big top;
A booking office for the circus,
And a gift, and souvenir shop.

Other travellers in their vehicles,
Pitched around the field;
Access to their big white tent,
Was quite securely sealed.

The billboard said they'd stop a week,
Two performances every day;
Prices for admission,
Were prominently on display.

My mum and dad looked at the prices,
And said it was too dear,
But they'd save up all their pennies,
And take me the following year.

EXCITED

Little feet in slippers,
Peeping round the door,
To see Santa's presents
On the floor.

Eyes open wide,
In the dark he can see,
The piles of parcels
Beneath the tree.

Can't reach the switch
To turn on the light;
Mum and dad in bed,
It's still the night.

Run back upstairs,
Jump onto the bed;
Peer out of the window,
For Santa's sledge.

No sign… he's gone,
He's far away;
With Rudolph pulling
His laden sleigh.

He'd eaten his mince pie,
Had a glass of wine,
No wonder he's fat,
Eating all the time.

Not long to wait
For mum and dad to wake;
Wish they'd hurry up,
For goodness sake.

Can't wait all day,
Why do they sleep so late?
They knew Santa was coming
On this Christmas date.

It's getting light,
Very nearly day,
Don't they know
That I need to play?

I'm sure there are toys,
In that great big stack;
How did he get so many
Into his sack?

Jump on their bed,
Shout and scream.
"Wake up mum
I think he's been."

Wipes sleep from her eyes,
Wishing there she could stay,
But she knows she's in for
A busy day!

STRAIGHT LACED

It's hard to do my shoes up,
No matter how I try.
I get hold of my shoelace,
Trying to pass it through the eye.

It's not like that with everything
When I have another go,
I can put my slippers on myself,
Because they have got velcro.

The elastic on my trainers,
Sometimes isn't right.
My finger acts as a shoe-horn,
But the fit is very tight.

I try the laces one more time,
And manage to get it through.
I'm proud of my achievement,
Cos I'm very nearly two!

Mummy says I'm learning,
I'm her bundle of joy.
When I can do my laces up,
I'll be a great big boy.

Soon I'll learn to read and write,
And then I'll go to school,
I'll be good at all my lessons,
I'll be nobody's fool!

But for now, I'll keep on trying,
To get those laces tied in bows.
My shoes can keep my feet warm,
From my ankles to my toes.

THE FACTS OF LIFE

"Where do babies come from?"
The question every parent dreads;
Searching for the right words,
In their muddled heads.

"They come from mummy's tummy,"
Is an answer that's not fair;
Because, the next thing that they want to know, is
How it got in there!

After much consideration,
And soul searching for what to say,
You sit the child down, quietly,
Thinking, "Let's get this out of the way."

"This is how you have babies,
Remember, before you could walk, or talk,
Mummy and daddy were visited
By a big white stork."

"It flew onto the rooftops,
It had a bag in its beak;
We found a little baby inside,
When we had a peek."

The child scratched his head and pondered,
He said, "If I was in that bag…
Does that mean mummy and daddy,
Didn't have a shag???"

THE ZOO

We went one day to the zoo,
We saw elephant, giraffes, and kangaroo;
There were lions and tigers, and big white bear,
And wild birds flying everywhere.

There were camels, that had got a hump,
And monkeys, with a bright red rump;
Zebras dressed in black and white stripes,
And bats, that only came out at night.

Macaw, parrot and cockatoo,
All trying to say "Hello" to you.
The snakes and alligators round a pool
Of stagnant water, to keep cool.

There was a hippopotamus up to his neck,
Mustn't touch the pelican, in case it pecks;
A day's not long enough, there's so much to do,
Can't wait to return again to the zoo.

SHINING EXAMPLE

One day, while sitting on the floor,
Your child was heard to say,
"Why is dad's head shiny?
But round the sides it's grey".

Another kid just piped up,
Completely out of the blue,
He spoke with such authority,
As though everybody knew.

He said, "His head is shiny,
But not around the edge,
I bet he rubs it every night,
Polishing it with Pledge."

"He's rubbed so hard his hair has gone,
Right across the middle;
Why he's got the side bits left,
Still remains a riddle."

When he asked directly,
This reply he got from you;
"My hair had to move out of the way,
To let the goodness all grow through!"

GREEN

The boy said, "Tell me, daddy,
Why's your hair all green?"
Dad sniffed, rubbed his palm across nose and head,
And said, "That's the way its always been."

He said, "I'm always sniffling,
I think it's flu I've got;
That's why the hair at the front of my head,
Is always full of snot!"

TAKEN FOR A RIDE

In the Summer, we went for a ride
In daddy's motor car;
Didn't know where we were going,
But it seemed to be quite far.

We looked out of the windows,
At the country scene;
Couldn't remember the names of the roads,
To know where we had been.

Wondering when he was going to stop,
He said, "You'll have to wait and see,"
I told him it had better be soon,
I was bursting for a wee.

Then I recognised a sign or two,
Though, they are all quite similar;
I knew this area very well,
The shops all looked familiar.

He turned into the street where we live,
And reversed into our drive;
He said he only wanted to try it out,
By going for a little ride.

FIRST DATE

Dating a girl for the very first time,
By the lampost on the street;
You asked her if she'd go out with you,
And that was a good place to meet.

You went along with a couple of mates,
And offered her a sweet;
Then told your friends to leave you alone,
You wanted to be discreet.

You stood and talked for quite a while,
She constantly flicked her hair;
You offered her a second sweet,
Said you had some to spare.

Your friends weren't very far away,
Giggling, and watching your action;
They thought they'd get some tips from you,
At least, criticise your reaction.

You don't know what they expected,
You only talked for a while;
Then you heard your mummy call you,
And she gave you a great big smile.

She said she'd like to see you again,
Same place would be just great;
Next time, don't bring along all those friends,
Because you know we're only eight!

BICYCLES

When you got your very first bike,
It had stabilisers at the rear;
Tassels hanging from the hand grips,
And a bell to keep folk clear.

The saddle was nicely padded,
It had a brightly coloured frame;
You'd let nobody else get near it,
If it got damaged, there was no one to blame.

Remember getting on it?
Trying to stay up straight?
Daddy letting go of the saddle,
As you crashed into the gate?

Once you'd mastered riding it,
The stabilisers were thrown away;
You'd never need them, ever again,
Starting from this day.

The bikes got bigger in the course of time,
Spread over the next ten years;
Til you ended up with a mountain bike,
With suspension, and twenty gears.

You still love going out for a ride,
But now you can go for miles;
When you think back to those early days,
Your face breaks into a smile.

MUSICAL CHAIRS

The party favourite of most kids,
Is the game of musical chairs;
It's the one where somebody jumps on your lap,
And catches you unawares.

The chairs form a line along the room,
Some facing this way, some facing that;
You skip and dance to the music,
Round the chairs while having a chat!

The talk acts as a form of distraction,
To all the others, at the hop;
You then set your eyes on an empty seat,
As soon as the music stops.

There's not enough chairs to go around,
Those unlucky are out of the game;
Then a seat is removed; the music restarts,
And off you go again.

The last one sitting is the winner,
Though you could be bruised and battered;
But beating all those other kids,
Is all that really mattered.

STORIES

Little tables, little chairs,
A blackboard, and white chalk;
Sit quietly, facing teacher,
You'll get told off if you talk.

Halfway through the morning,
You are told to fold your arms;
While teacher reads a story,
About life down on the farm.

You listen quite intently,
Making noises when you're told;
Mimicking the animals,
From the field, or in the fold.

Then, when you are asked questions,
You're encouraged to raise your hand;
Why you can't shout the answer,
You'll never understand.

Tomorrow is another day,
So she'll read from another book;
But I've already heard that tale before,
I sneaked to her desk, and looked.

I recognised the pictures,
Printed on the page;
But I couldn't read the squiggly words,
Not at my tender age!

THE POTATO

He planted a potato in his garden,
Just like his daddy said;
He put it in a hole he'd dug,
In the flower bed.

For months he kept an eye on it,
Leaves formed, then a white flower;
He waited, and he waited,
For hour, on hour, on hour.

When his dad said it was ready,
To dig the lonely spud,
He gave the boy a little fork,
To dig down in the mud.

There were lots of small potatoes,
All white amongst the soil;
The look upon his little face,
Was well worth all that toil.

The boy looked up at daddy,
As his eye shed a little tear;
"I think I love you daddy,
I'll grow one for you next year."

PLEASE RELEASE ME

The budgerigar was talking,
As he sat in his cage;
Balanced on his little perch,
Watched by a lad of young age.

The cage was on the sideboard,
When the bird began to sing;
He was blue, with spots around his throat,
On his leg he wore a ring.

The boy looked on in amazement,
As it washed in its drinking pot;
Then hopped again onto its perch
Which was peppered with black and white dots.

"I think he wants to go out,
He's got his jewellery in place;
He's already started singing,
And he's washed his little face."

"If I open the door to his cage,
He can go on his way."
But, mummy's voice came from the kitchen,
"You do, and there'll be hell to pay!"

PIGGY BANK

He stuck a knife in his piggy bank,
Coins fell to the floor;
Then he decided to shake it,
To see if it contained any more.

He scooped up all the pennies,
And went to the corner shop;
Laid the money on the counter,
And asked how much he'd got.

The lady counted all his coins,
And said how much he had;
A tear formed in his little eye,
And his face looked rather sad.

"I wanted a present for my mummy,
And thought I had enough to pay.
She'd like a box of chocolates,
For tomorrow it's her birthday."

The lady felt quite sorry,
For the little lad;
Gave him a big box of chocolates,
But only charged him the money he had.

ALWAYS QUESTIONS

You're always asking questions,
What; When; Where; Why; Who?
I think you're getting nosey,
Its got nothing to do with you.

Why don't you mind your own business?
If it concerns you, you'll be told;
Until that day, just go away,
Try to be as good as gold.

I think that it's important,
That children know their place;
But, asking all those questions,
Is an absolute disgrace.

"Let me stay here, daddy,
Please don't make me go;
If I can't ask any questions,
How will I ever know?"

"I can't learn everything from books,
The Internet, or TV.
The reason I ask you questions,
Is the love you have for me."

"I know you don't really mean it,
When my curiosity gets in your way;
But if I can keep asking questions,
Maybe I'll be brainy some day!"

SPORTS DAY

Taking part in the egg and spoon race,
Is a must for every child;
With the egg balanced nicely in the bowl,
The crowd go really wild.

Then you're given a sack to put on,
The two corners are best for your feet;
It leaves plenty of room to run along,
So you probably won't get beat.

A ribbon is strung across the track,
To act as a finishing line;
The children, from the starting gun,
See who can run in the fastest time.

The mum's race is always a favourite,
And the children hide their sniggers;
For when the mums' fall over,
They sometimes show their knickers.

NIT NURSE

A lady in a white coat,
Took us one by one into a room;
She said to all those waiting,
"I'll be with you soon."

She asked our names then ticked a box,
Said, "Sit down on that chair,"
Then put on a pair of rubber gloves,
And rummaged in our hair.

She knew she wasn't popular,
But didn't seem to mind;
She had to look down to the scalp,
To see what she could find.

If she found a trace of head lice,
She'd send a message to your home;
Mum would have to buy a special shampoo,
And a little metal comb.

They called her Nitty Nora,
And she visited once a year;
I said, "You don't need to look in my hair,
You'll find nothing crawling here!"

PANTO

Once, I had a lovely surprise,
Organised by my dad's firm;
They took us to the pantomime,
Right at the end of term.

They led us into the theatre,
Allocated us all seats;
Then, one of the ladies working there,
Gave us all a bag of sweets.

The play was very colourful,
And we were prompted by the crew,
To call out, when we saw a man,
"He's there… right behind you!!!"

I think the other man was stupid,
He said, "Oh no he's not!"
We all called back, "Oh yes he is!"
As they got on with the plot.

I think that actors must be gay,
I'll give them six marks out of ten;
For lead boy was played by a lady,
The ugly sisters were all men.

FITTED UP

They stand in the school outfitters shop,
In front of a mirror, trying on blazers;
Kitted out by their doting parents,
Too young to use shaving razors.

Rosy red cheeks, aglow and rotund,
Trying trousers to find the right size;
The podgy offspring, with forty inch waist,
Material clinging to their thighs.

The blazer would fit the father,
Sufficient material to go round the chest;
The pristine white shirt, and striped school tie,
Covering the boy's pendulent breasts.

A rugby shirt in the school's colours,
And shorts, not stretched at the seams,
Big enough, when held up in the air,
To take the rest of the team.

A diet and exercise is called for,
To prevent the child getting called names;
Trying to lose a few pounds of fat,
Running it off during school games.

But the regime mustn't stop at the end of school,
It must also continue at home;
Parents must control the intake of their sons,
It's no excuse to say, "He's just big-boned".

THE SUPERMARKET

When we go to the supermarket,
Mummy sits me in the trolley;
I use the space that's next to me,
To sit my favourite dolly.

We travel up and down the store,
Picking up what we need;
Sometimes we buy lots of fruit,
And maybe a packet of seed.

Daddy plants them in the garden,
But they never seem to grow;
Why he really bothers,
I will never know.

When we've finished shopping,
We'll head for an empty till;
You can guarantee we've got the trolley,
That's got a wobbly wheel.

We usually pay by credit card,
Then put the shopping in the car;
It's better than getting on buses,
And takes less time by far.

I'm grateful that my dolly,
Never says a word;
But with her sitting next to me,
It stops me getting bored.

GREEN APPLE

An apple fell down on the ground,
From the branches of a tree;
It was a great big green one,
That landed in-front of me.

I picked it up, and looked it over,
And as far as I was aware;
Nothing was wrong with the shiny fruit,
It was big enough to share.

I took it home, and cut it up,
Into tiny little bits;
I gave a piece each to mum and dad,
Who took out all the pips.

Then, in mine I saw a movement,
Something wriggling, in my piece;
My parents hadn't touched theirs,
So I said, "Yummy… what a feast."

With that, they started eating,
Then mum's scream cut into the calm;
I don't know what she's worried about,
Maggots don't do fish any harm.

KITES

Flying a kite is special,
As it soars up in the air;
Floated by the gust of wind,
As though it hasn't got a care.

You tug the string to make it jump,
It twists, and forms somersaults in the sky;
Sometimes, it won't get off the ground,
No matter how much you try.

Occasionally, the string gets twisted,
At least that's what I've found;
So if the kite won't do as it's told,
It'll crash into the ground.

It's good playing with a kite,
Trying to keep it in the air;
Wrapped up warm on top of a hill,
The wind blowing through your hair.

It's not for the faint-hearted,
Who don't like to be outdoors;
Kite flying won't do much for them,
And will be one of their biggest bores.

DADDY LONG LEGS

If you see a daddy long legs,
In the corner of the room;
Make a noise… really loud,
And it'll scamper back into the gloom.

But if you want to catch one,
No matter how long, or tall;
You're better off if it is deaf,
It won't hear you creeping along the hall.

A way to carry out this task,
Performed by kids throughout the years,
For some reason, leaves their parents
Very close to tears.

All you really need to do,
Is pull its legs off…one by one;
Then, no matter how much you call it,
I guarantee it'll never come.

I don't know why it works that way,
But the creature cannot hear;
Or it'd run away to its hiding place,
And wouldn't fill us with fear.

CONKERS

Conkers, collected from the ground,
Taken from their prickly shell;
Keeping all the big ones,
They're winners I can tell.

Dry them out, and pickle them,
In a vinegar pot;
Bake others in the oven,
Make them really hot.

It's supposed to make them difficult,
When you play the game,
To break, when they've been seasoned,
Though they're usually just the same.

Always pick the best one,
Pierce a hole right through its core;
Thread it on some knotted string,
And you'll find challengers galore.

They'll all want to be the champion,
By smashing yours to bits;
Don't let them take advantage,
By having too many hits.

If you are not a winner,
Don't cry if it drives you bonkers;
After all, you're only playing a game,
And there's plenty more big conkers.

INJECTIONS

The nurse said, "Roll your shirt sleeve up,
I don't want to hear you whinge,"
Then, came at me across the surgery,
With a bloody great syringe.

She said it wouldn't hurt me,
It was just a little prick;
But the sight of her big instrument,
Made me feel quite sick.

I shut my eyes and grimaced,
She said, "Now stay real calm,"
She rubbed a swab upon my skin,
And stuck the needle in my arm.

I couldn't avoid the injection,
No matter how I tried;
But it didn't hurt me that much,
Cos I never even cried.

POTTY TRAINING

He pulled his little trousers down,
Way below his knees;
Then his tiny underpants,
And said, "I want the potty please."

It was all part of his training,
As he said he wants a poo;
He sat there several minutes,
Trying to push one through.

Then, he proudly said he'd finished,
And stood up from the pot;
Grabbed handfuls of the toilet roll,
And wiped his little bot.

Mum made him wash his dirty hands,
At the kitchen sink;
The only thing she couldn't do,
Was get rid of the stink.

THE FUTURE

Children playing,
Throwing balls;
Doing handstands
Against walls.

Run and jump,
Through skipping ropes;
Their young lives
Full of hopes.

In the playground,
Playing chase;
And rounders,
Getting back to base.

Kicking footballs,
Coats for goals;
Wembley Stadium
For imaginative souls.

Our future government
Starts right here;
Before political life
Kicks into gear.

Business empires
Will be found,
Starting in that
School playground.

Let children play
As long as can be;
For they're the future
Of our country.

Section 9

"SSSSH!"...I'M WRITING

UNINSPIRED

I tried to write a poem,
Just a couple of lines,
I jotted down some random words,
But nothing seemed to rhyme.

I needed inspiration,
I was looking for a sign,
To get me motivated,
But nothing… not a line.

I threw away so much paper,
With abandoned "Works of Art".
What was missing most of all,
Was knowing how to start.

I didn't have a beginning,
A middle or conclusion.
My mind was in a muddle,
Filled with such confusion.

I wanted to send the finished verse
To "Connect", to fill a page,
But how can you send unfinished work,
That's lacking in so many ways.

I guess I'll have to leave it,
Apologise to Emily,
For taking up so much of her time,
There's nothing here to see!

CHANGING COLOURS

The traffic lights changed from amber to red,
As the cars came to a halt.
Pedestrians crossed on the studded path,
Without giving others a thought.

They pushed, and shoved to get across,
Before the man changed from green.
Their obsession to get there before the rest,
Was quite literally obscene.

No regard for anyone but themselves,
They don't care who gets in the way.
Anyone left in the middle of the road,
When the lights changed... there they stay.

Red and amber appear, and the cars start to move,
They don't wait for the people to clear.
Anyone left in the middle of the road,
Would be filled with a sense of fear.

It's quite a challenge to see who'll win,
In the race to clear the lights first.
The pedestrians can run to get out of the way,
But the car's engines rev up, fit to burst.

I'd hate to be crossing against the flow,
of the others in this tide.
I'd never make headway against the throng,
So I guess I'll stay on this side!!

Ssssh! …I'M WRITING

I can't stop writing these poems,
The words just come in my mind.
Some people struggle with phrases,
But I don't think they're hard to find.

The words seem to link together,
To tell a story or two.
A slightly embellished account, perhaps,
But basically the tale is true.

I need a few facts at first though,
So if someone's situation is a joke,
Just tell me their name and circumstance,
Then for fun we can have a poke!

I'll try to write it as it happened,
Exaggeration is a must,
To keep the reader's mind amused,
And giggling fit to bust.

Some bits I write are serious,
And they do not evoke humour,
But I like to lighten the tale, and so
I inject a suspicion of rumour.

I don't want to offend anybody,
So I won't write anything blue,
But if you think I could write you a rhyme,
Then I'd like to hear from you.

A to Z

I've always found the dictionary
A fascinating book,
You can pick it up at anytime,
Select a page, and take a look.

It doesn't have a story
That you need to follow through.
You can open it at any page,
And find a word that's new.

If I take the book I've got to hand,
And open it at the "A" section,
I spy the word that's spelt ALATE,
Meaning "Wings, or a winglike erection."

The "B"s, reveal BALNEARY,
Which sounds to me, quite scathing.
But when I read the script attached,
It applies to, "baths, and bathing".

CLERIHEW, jumps out from the pages for "C",
Writing like this can be a curse.
For the dictionary says it's" comical,
Portrayed in a short, witty verse."

Under "D", we find DALTONISM,
Of colour blindness, it must be said.
The person who suffers from this disease,
"Can't distinguish green from red."

ENCAUSTIC, is a form of painting,
Found with the "E"s, of which there are stacks.
It uses different coloured clays,
Burnt in, and sealed with wax."

Under "F", we come across FACULA,
A word relating to Astronomy.
It's a "streak, or a bright spot on the sun."
That is there, for all to see.

We turn the pages, and come to "G",
So after a little while,
We find the passage for GAVIAL,
"A long nosed, Asian crocodile."

I thought that HALLUX, would be a word,
That under "H", I should know.
But it's "a digit on the hind foot,
Or in humans, it's the big toe."

The pages for "I", give us IMBRICATE,
And it's found looking through the files.
It means "having scales, for example,
Arranged to overlap, like tiles."

JACARANDA, is a tree of scented wood,
In America, above all, it towers.
It dwarfs the trees within its shade,
"And has trumpet shaped, blue flowers."

"A fabulous, composite animal,
on Chinese pottery", found therein.
When looking under the letter "K",
We come across KYLIN.

A LABRET, is a "piece of bone,
Or could be a bit of shell.
Used as a facial ornament,"
And can be in the lips as well.

Under "M", we find the word MARKHOR,
In Northern India, this is born.
"The genus is a wild goat,
That has a long, spiral horn."

NOVENA, consists of "special prayer,

70

In a service of devoted ways.
Used by the Roman Catholic Church,
It's for nine successive days."

We look within "O", and find a word,
That looks from a different class.
OBSIDIAN, stands out from the page,
And is "a rock, like bottle-glass."

If ever you're in Italy,
And want a " ewe-milk cheese,"
Just ask for PECARINO,
You'll get one that will please.

A QUAGGA, is a quadruped,
"Related to zebra and ass."
It was found in Southern Africa,
But is now extinct, alas.

I've got to "R", and for a moment,
Thought that I would falter.
Until I found REREDOS was,
"A screen at the back of the Altar."

"A dry fruit, that splits open when ripe,
into seeded parts, that are quite sharp,"
Are in the section under "S",
Listed as SCHIZOCARP.

A TARBOOSH, is a "type of cap,
That looks like a fez in Egypt.
Sometimes, it is worn all alone,
Or with a turban," it's quite hip!

Eskimo women use a boat,
"With paddles, they steer it good,"
They call this boat a UMIAK,
"It's made from skins and wood."

Under "V", we find a nautical word,
VANG, is a "kind of rope.

It runs from end of gaff to the deck,"
So that those on board can cope.

When I look under the "W"s,
Instantly, I spy WASSERMAN.
"It's a test for identifying syphilis,
Using the patient's reaction to serum."

XANTHOMA, is "a skin disease,
That doctors can detect.
It leaves irregular patches,
Round the throat, and on the neck."

If you were a "Mongolian nomad,
That had a collapsible frame.
Supporting a tent made only from skin,"
A YOORT, would be its name.

ZYMURGY, is the last word in this book.
"Fermentation Chemistry, used in brewing,"
The knowledge we've gained by writing this ode,
is gradually accruing.

If I look back through the book again,
I could find a lot more on the pages.
To read, digest, and memorise,
That would pass the time for ages.

Now, I'll summarise my findings,
The words I've chosen, they do vary.
But every one of these you'll find,
In the Concise Oxford Dictionary.

LUNARTIC

My wife bought me a telescope,
To look up at the stars.
To focus in on Saturn,
On Jupiter and Mars.

It's a big thing on a tripod,
And kept in the spare room.
Pointing up towards the sky,
For looking at the moon.

It's difficult to focus,
Because the stars look very small.
Sometimes, I can't see one,
In fact, I can't see much at all!

The moon is quite a big thing,
Shining in the sky,
The only thing to look at,
If I really try.

I put one eye to the eyepiece,
Trying not to knock the stand.
I shut the other one to help
Me see this cosmic land.

The moon looks kind of fuzzy,
With craters on its face.
You expect to see a rocket land,
In the N.A.S.A. race.

After a while of looking,
I start to lose my patience,
'Cos nothing seems to happen,
In this race amongst the nations.

When you've looked at one moon,
I think you've seen them all.
There isn't much to look at,
Just a big white ball.

DETECTION

While on holiday one year,
I took my metal detector to a field.
I started walking, up and down,
To see what it would yield.

I was wearing my new headphones,
And was carrying a trowel.
I had to wear my wellies,
The weather was pretty foul.

It wasn't long before I heard,
A bleeping sound in my head-set.
I grabbed my trowel, and started digging,
Into soil that was extremely wet.

I sifted through the turned up dirt,
Scraping with my hands.
Breaking up the clods of mud,
The making of the land.

The hole was getting rather deep,
I'd gone down about a foot.
Still, my detector registered,
That I'd found some long lost loot.

I felt something round within the mud,
I was a very excited man.
Until I saw it was a ring-pull,
From a Coca-Cola can.

I continued with my searching,
It didn't put me off my cause,
I wandered up and down the field,
I didn't even pause.

That day, I found a lot of bits,
Deterred? not in the least.
After rejecting all of those ring-pulls,
I found a two-pence piece.

When metal objects are detected,
You don't know what's in store.
Until you've unearthed just what it is,
Then you'll want to look for more.

It's really quite addictive,
You just can't get enough.
Not knowing what's beneath your feet,
Even when the weather's rough.

DISGRUNTLED CONTENDERS

I'll always support the underdog,
In a football match.
When the goalie rushes out of the box,
And tries to make a catch.

The forwards struggle to get the ball,
They are completely outclassed.
The defence is always in disarray,
And they really can't be arsed!

The players stop running, when the ball is kicked,
When they jump to head... it's far too early.
They land back on their feet before the ball arrives,
They play the game, sort of "girlie".

When the whistle blows, they just can't wait
To get into the showers.
They've only been playing for ninety minutes,
But it feels like ninety hours.

A heavy defeat, again, to record,
Another resounding blow,
To the struggling team that can't win games,
And has no points to show.

The opposition is always better,
They score lots of goals, classed as "lucky".
But you've got to admit for the underdogs,
Facing defeat each week... they're plucky!

PSITTACOSIS

Some time ago, my garage
Was partitioned down the middle.
Neighbours wondered what I was doing,
To them it was a riddle.

In the wall at the end, I made a hole,
By taking out some bricks.
They looked on in amazement,
As I got up to my tricks.

But round the back they couldn't see,
For it was out of sight.
I'd built a cage with wire mesh,
To use it as a flight.

Back inside the garage,
I installed a few nest boxes,
To complete my little aviary,
And protect it from the foxes.

I started with a few budgerigars,
In white, and blue, and green.
To see them flying in the cage,
Was surely a sight to be seen.

One day, I found that one of them,
Had laid an egg, quite small.
I waited weeks for it to hatch,
It was white, and looked quite dull.

I eagerly kept an eye on it,
Waiting for it to hatch,
When I found yet another egg,
From a different batch.

This fleshy little thing appeared,
With not a feather in sight.
Wriggling, in the nest box,
Struggling with all its might.

I bought other budgies over the months,
To add to those already there.
The eggs were laid frequently, in several boxes,
As the birds separated into pairs.

The sight of the babies, when feathers appeared,
Was, for me, a dream come true.
I've always dreamed of hatching eggs out,
And it had come out of the blue.

I then became adventurous,
So I bought a pair of cockatiels.
A much larger bird for the aviary,
Whose appearance filled me with thrills.

Grey in colour, with a yellow flash
On either side of their heads,
They needed much larger nest boxes,
And sunflower seeds, were fed.

I always kept an eye on them,
And it was obvious they were ready for breeding.
Until, one day, I noticed an egg in their box,
So I supplied anything they were needing.

I wanted the egg to hatch on time,
So I bought books, of which to read.
I studied the gestation period,
And read up on all they might need.

One day, when inspecting the nest box,
I noticed something was missing.
The egg had gone, but had been replaced,
By a fluffy thing, that was hissing.

The chick had a covering of very fine hair,
And held its head up high.
The hissing sound, I got used to,
But to touch it... I dare not try.

The parents flapped around nearby,
Very protective of their young.
Whenever I went near the box,
They'd burst into a frenzied song.

I tried to keep some finches,
To mix with the other birds.
I didn't find this quite so enjoyable,
But couldn't put it into words.

Wherever I put bird seed,
Much of it would drop.
So I placed a tray beneath it,
Inside the garage, to catch a lot.

I filled the tray with peat and soil,
So they could land, and scratch about,
Then I introduced a few Japanese quail,
Who would rummage, and sort it all out.

The downside was that it attracted mice,
Til I had more mice than birds.
Occasionally, one got into the house,
And my wife shouted a few choice words!

Unfortunately, about that time,
I managed to get pneumonia.
I was taken to hospital for quite a time,
Then at home for months, to recover.

They said the cause of my infection,
Was the dust carried in the bird's feathers,
And suggested I get rid of them,
To ensure that I got better.

They told me that psittacosis,
Can be transferred in all aspects.
It affects the lungs, and breathing,
Causing respiratory defects.

Reluctantly, I did just that,
And my garage was used for the car.
The flight, and nest boxes were pulled down,
And, better use of the space made, by far.

I don't think I'll ever attempt it again,
Although, I can say I've given it a try.
Keeping birds is one thing,
But I don't really want to die!

SPOONERISM'S

The Reverend W.A. Spooner
Passed away in 1930.
But he left behind a legacy,
That some people treat as dirty.

He was an English scholar,
Who made errors in his speech,
He unwittingly twisted words around,
Confusing those that chose to teach.

The initial letters of words he used,
Were accidentally, or deliberately transposed.
And that is how the term used today,
"Spoonerism" became exposed.

One example that occurred during teaching,
Said he'd "Hissed the Mystery Lesson".
Nobody understood what he meant,
But he'd "Missed the History session".

Another came when he was asked to explain,
About a half-formed wish,
He couldn't get his words out right,
And spoke of a half-warmed fish.

But, I think the best one I ever heard,
On the news, they spoke of the West Bank.
I'll leave you to work out what was said,
So, this last line reads, "Blankety-Blank".

FAITH, HOPE AND GLORY

Rooney's back on the World Cup scene,
He's been assessed on his foot today.
He'll probably take part in a couple of weeks,
Following group matches, he'll start to play.

They say his broken metatarsal,
Is mending really well.
But only when he's played a game,
Will the medics finally tell.

He's working OK in training,
His comeback is going to plan.
But we'd like his return to the first team squad,
Just as quick as he can.

We've got a chance without him,
'Cos one man doesn't make a team.
But his replacement, Crouch, is like an octopus,
All arms and legs it seems!

No, we really do need Rooney,
Let's hope he plays a part,
In hammering all those foreign teams,
Giving English fans new heart.

Who knows? When he's back in the team,
And our prospects are looking up,
Perhaps we'll believe we've got a chance,
Of winning the 2006 World Cup.

AVIAN INFLUENZA

As the birds fly into Britain,
And they migrate in their flock,
We hear the news we've been dreading,
Though it doesn't come as a shock.

The first case of bird flu has been confirmed,
In a little Scottish port,
Where a swan was found in the harbour,
Its carcass floating until it was caught.

It took a few days, til the news was released,
Now it's in the papers, and on the telly.
It's been confirmed, that what was feared,
Once they examined the inside of the swan's belly.

They call the virus H5N-ONE,
Its travelled to us from the East.
Where there's been reports of it spreading,
Through birds, to man and beast.

An exclusion zone around the port,
Has limited people's movements.
They disinfect boots, and vehicles alike,
In the hope of it showing improvement.

Local farmers are told to keep their birds indoors,
Away from any airborne invasion.
They may be clear of this avian strain,
But could cause havoc and devastation.

The Environment Agency has issued reports,
Saying that birds are still OK to eat.
There's really no need to panic,
As long as you cook any eggs and meat.

The Health Department has made an announcement,
That humans have nothing to fear.
There's a minute risk, but not in excess,
Of anything else we face each year.

It's shown in Europe, that it can be passed on,
To cats that have eaten their prey.
When they've stalked, and caught, the birds in their sight,
That couldn't get out of their way.

There's no evidence to cause us to panic,
So the government has made a plea,
But we'll only know in the future,
So we'll just have to wait, and see!

MEDWAY... AND ALL ON OFFER!

If you leave the train at Rochester or Chatham,
The area looks pretty bleak.
But spend some time to look around,
And you'll want to stay for a week.

There's plenty on offer for everyone,
For young and old alike.
Regeneration is taking place,
Whether you use train, bus, car or bike!

There are plans to build a cable car,
To traverse the water up high,
To soar above the river walks,
Sailing through the sky.

Rochester's castle and beautiful grounds,
On the River Medway's bank;
Overlooking the bridge and marina,
For this we have the Normans to thank.

There's another castle at Upnor,
That guarded the ships of Queen Elizabeth the First.
Built in 1559,
I think any invaders would have come off worst.

A stone's throw from Rochester Castle,
Is the cathedral, standing so grand.
Built in 604, by Bishop Justus,
It's the second oldest in the land.

Over 400 years of naval history,
When the dockyard built great ships;
It's now open to the public, with static displays,
Exhibitions, and even boat trips.

The "Kingswear Castle" is a paddle steamer,
The last in Britain, fired by coal.
Giving Summer rides along the river,
An adventure for young and old.

Fort Amhurst, in Chatham, is a Napoleonic fort,
Built into the hillside.
Overlooking and protecting the dockyard,
Open to visitors, with an experienced guide.

Military history dominates the towns,
So to see tanks and guns and more;
The Royal Engineer's Museum in Brompton
Will have you flocking to its door.

If you're more attracted to civil events,
Then Rochester won't be a failure.
The Guildhall Museum in the High Street,
Houses all of the town's regalia.

The outdoor life is catered for,
With numerous country parks to roam.
Through Rainham and Gillingham, to Capstone Farm,
Plus Ranscombe Farm Reserve, nearer to home.

There's an outdoor swimming pool, if you wish,
Located at the Strand Leisure Park.
Numerous indoor pools scattered throughout the towns,
Catering for all, til way after dark.

For those that like to take a stroll,
And admire the floral displays;
Jackson's playing fields in Rochester,
Will be the highlight of your day.

Anyone who likes to dress the part,
Will adore Rochester's contribution.
The Sweep's Festival is held the Mayday weekend,
And has become a regular institution.

Morris dancers and musicians perform in the streets,
Their dress covered in soot and feathers.
A photographer's dream, if you visit the scene,
It goes ahead whatever the weather.

For many years now, there's been a festival,
Surrounding the life and times of Charles Dickens,
With processions by people in character dress,
And a funfair in the castle gardens.

The Chinese New Year is celebrated in Chatham,
With traditional dragons, on display.
Not the usual find in a Medway street,
But making a very enjoyable day!

If you're still in need of entertainment,
There's plenty for you to see.
Visiting artists at the Central Theatre,
For a very nominal fee.

The Summer months come into their own,
With a week of musical concerts in store.
Big named stars appearing in the castle gardens,
Leave you clamouring for more.

Tickets are always hard to obtain,
Because they sell out very fast.
Once you've gained admission, to see these events,
I guarantee, it won't be your last!!!

With all of this going on in Medway,
There's no way you could get bored with events,
Whatever your taste in pastimes,
The facilities are heaven sent.

So, to all at the local council,
Who put these events together;
You've got a wonderful selection,
For any kind of weather.

As for the town's regeneration,
It's a long term plan, indeed.
But now the Riverside clearance has started,
I'm sure that you WILL succeed.

The artist's impressions look adventurous,
To say the very least,
But when it's all completed,
The facilities will be a feast.

You'll never please everybody,
The traffic upheaval will become a pain;
But don't forget those visitors,
That just got off that train.

Like I said, in my opening verses,
Round the stations it appears quite dour.
But once you start looking around you,
You'll be mesmerised within the hour.

Well done... to Medway Council,
You're making us feel quite proud.
Instead of criticising your actions,
I think we should applaud you... out loud!!!

FOOTBALL CRAZY

2006 is a World Cup year,
For football lovers, everywhere.
In '66 the Germans came here,
But this year, it's over there!

For months, the fans have gone crazy,
Flying flags from houses and cars.
The build-up has been tremendous,
Business booming in pubs and bars.

Gigantic screens are erected,
To appeal to supporters, from all walks of life.
To give them the opportunity,
To watch – with or without their wife!

Lots of women take no interest,
In all the fuss that's taking place.
They'd rather stay at home with their family,
Their husband, vanished, without a trace.

Four weeks of non-stop matches,
From all of the teams that qualified.
Lots have fallen by the wayside,
But they can always say they tried.

Every English fan talks of '66,
When the Finals were played, and won.
Wembley Stadium hosting the prestigious match,
In the heat of the July sun.

We've been talking about that sensational win,
Continuously, for the past forty years.
When Hurst and Peters scored four goals,
And Germany's hopes ended in tears.

We can't always dwell in the past though,
This year we've got to score more than the rest.
To win all the matches thrown at us,
To prove that we're still the best.

Let's hope the fans can support their country,
Boost their chances, and lift them up.
So, on the 9th Of July, at 9 pm.
David Beckham will lift the World Cup.

A treat for all of the country,
A spectacle, for all to see.
Let's hope that we're victorious,
And the events are trouble- free!

IT'S ANNOYING

Drip.
The tap is dripping.
It makes a new sound every time.
Drip.
It still keeps dripping.
The rhythm sounds just fine.
Drip, drip.
It's getting faster.
I think it's getting worse.
Drip, drip.
It's quite annoying.
I'm finding it difficult to converse.
Drip, drip, drip.
It's starting to aggravate me.
I wish I knew how to turn it off.
Drip, drip, drip.
I'm at the end of my tether.
I'd love to make it stop.

WE DIDN'T LOSE... WE WERE SECOND!

The reason we didn't win the game,
Isn't because we didn't score.
It's just that the opposition,
Scored a whole lot more!

Our goalie stood inside the net,
More times than on the line.
Retrieving the ball from his domain,
Restarting the game in record time.

The ref spent the time with his whistle,
Glued between his lips,
Pointing to the centre spot,
Our forwards could use some tips.

We spent our time running in circles,
Back pedalling, along the pitch.
Trying to hold the advancing crowd,
But it didn't go without a hitch.

They moved the ball from wing to wing,
Sometimes high up in the air.
Their passing was immaculate,
They controlled it everywhere.

I think we were the better team,
Even though we lost.
We earned that orange, shared between us,
Adding to our overhead costs.

At least our shirts looked better,
After the game, they still looked white.
They were plastered in mud on the opposing team,
Their's were a horrible sight.

The ball very rarely came near us,
So we didn't get dirty kit.
At least we'll save on the Persil,
As our manager sees fit.

I suppose there has to be a loser,
So I think we've played our part.
Without us, there wouldn't be a winner,
And the game just couldn't start.

So… here's to losers everywhere,
We all owe you a favour,
But holding up that trophy,
Is something you will never savour!

CIRCULARS

Another load of leaflets,
Had been put through the door.
Landing on the carpet,
Scattering across the floor.

They're very seldom looked at,
Most go into the bin;
With every free newspaper,
You'll find lots are tucked within.

There's bathrooms and double glazing,
And Indian Takeaways,
Aids for the disabled,
To help them ease their days.

They should try to save the paper,
Because I think they felled a tree,
To accumulate such a huge amount,
Like they have sent to me!

OFF ROAD BIKERS

They race across the playing fields,
In groups of two, three, or four.
While sometimes, at holidays and weekends,
It's possible to get lots more.

They rev the engines on their bikes,
Making lots of noise.
They're a nuisance to the residents,
Those men, and girls, and boys.

There are mopeds ridden by little kids,
Teenagers, and adults alike,
Scooters are used for doing stunts,
While some ride trials, and even quad bikes.

They seldom wear a crash helmet,
As they speed across the grass,
There's going to be an accident,
They're going much too fast.

Three on a bike's not unusual,
For kids aged about eleven.
Oblivious to any dangers,
It's their idea of heaven!

The police say they won't allow them,
To ride on the open space,
But that's a challenge to the kids,
Who want somewhere to race.

When the police do make an appearance,
The bikers scatter amongst the trees.
They very rarely catch anyone,
Despite the council's pleas.

They say the fields are for families,
And for football matches to take place.
Somewhere for people to walk their dogs,
Riding motorbikes is in very bad taste.

But for the bikers, there is nowhere to go,
Nowhere to ride, or meet.
So they congregate on the playing fields,
After riding through the streets.

The police said in the local press,
"Somebody must take the bikes there, by van,"
They think these kids obey the rules,
But they'll ride through the streets if they can.

They tear along the narrow roads,
Through estates, and footpaths alike.
They don't worry about motorists, or pedestrians,
Their aim… just to ride their bikes.

These bikes are quite expensive,
When they are legally bought.
Some parents spending lots of cash,
Without giving the law a thought.

They've been known to ride across football pitches,
While matches are being played,
Scaring the life out of the kiddies teams,
And making them feel afraid.

Very often, when the sun goes down,
And sometimes, late at night,
We'll be woken by the fire brigade,
Where a stolen bike has been set alight.

The council remove the burnt out wrecks,
That leave blackened patches on the grass,
The kids will steal another one,
And I'm sure it won't be their last!

They have no inhibitions,
No thought for possessions, or someone's transport.
That somebody can't get to work, next day,
Because they've now lost the bike they'd bought.

If there's nowhere legal for them to ride,
Without fear of confiscation,
They're going to terrorise neighbourhoods,
In towns throughout the nation.

I have an idea, one way to control them,
Is to build towers, half concealed.
Each tower is armed with machine-guns,
At the corners of the field!!!

That'll sort the buggers out,
They won't ride there no more!
Then the council can send the lorry round,
To pick the machines up from the floor.

CORRIE

When Coronation Street first appeared on our screens,
It was all in black and white,
I was still a young boy at school,
It was on, Monday and Wednesday nights.

Minnie Caldwell and Martha Longhurst,
With Ena Sharples, in the snug
Of the Rovers Return, on the cobbled street,
That the nation grew to love.

Elsie Tanner was played by Pat Phoenix,
A battleaxe, a real man-eater.
There was always a string of fella's
Calling round to meet her.

Peter Adamson played Len Fairclough,
Who was always a bit of a card.
A likeable sort of bloke in the street,
Who ran a builder's yard.

He met a girl named Rita,
Who sang on the nightclub circuit.
Eventually, they married,
And everything seemed perfect.

Len went into partnership with Ray Langton,
In the building trade.
Ray met, and married Deidre,
After several advances he'd made.

Stan and Hilda Ogden, were an ordinary pair,
They had a "murial" on their wall,
With a set of three flying ducks,
One of which was about to fall.

Ken Barlow was the brother of David,
Whose parents were Ida and Frank.
When he started, he was only a young lad,
Who was sometimes up for a prank.

Ken's uncle was Albert Tatlock,
Who lived in his terraced home,
He always seemed a miserable chap,
And ready for a moan.

The Rovers was run by Annie Walker,
Assisted by her husband, Jack.
For the Newton and Ridley brewery,
With deliveries, made round the back.

Len Fairclough's son was called Stanley,
And was played by Peter Noone.
He later joined Herman's Hermits,
Making the girls in the 60s swoon.

The street's had lots of incidents,
With shootings, and stabbings galore.
A robbery at Baldwin's factory,
As Ernest Bishop made for the door.

The viaduct collapsed at one point,
And the factory's been burnt down.
There's been a lot more deaths in this street,
Than in any northern town.

Harry Hewitt was killed under his car,
When it fell off of the jack,
It pinned him to the pavement,
Breaking every bone in his back.

The stories cover every type of topic,
From teenage births, and abortions,
To homosexual relationships,
All calling on your emotions.

When Deidre was jailed, several years ago,
It made news in the National Press.
The storyline really got out of hand,
Until she was released when her accuser confessed.

Mike Baldwin had fights with Ken Barlow,
And he gave him a couple of shiners,
While fighting for the love of Deidre,
But now, he's suffering from Alzheimer's.

It's been forty years since it started,
Bill Roache was in it from the start,
With his role as boring Ken Barlow,
Quite a well acted part.

These days it's on several times a week,
And the cast has changed a lot.
The scriptwriters do a fantastic job,
Giving many a twist to the plot.

Let's hope it continues for many more years,
And the storylines get stronger,
I've followed it now, for forty-odd years,
So I'm sure I can follow it longer.

ENGLAND'S 2006 CAMPAIGN

When they played against Paraguay,
England's best player was Joe Cole.
But, the only way they won the match,
Was with Paraguay's own goal.

Trinidad and Tobago were the following team,
The next game of this tour.
England managed to win it,
But their performance was pretty poor.

David Beckham crossed the ball,
But it wasn't a sure bet,
Until Peter Crouch jumped in the air,
And headed into the net.

A couple of minutes later,
The ball was struck quite hard,
From just outside the penalty box,
By Liverpudlian, Steve Gerrard.

Michael Owen was substituted again,
That's two matches in a row.
But for the last quarter of the match,
Sven let Wayne Rooney have a go.

They said his foot was better,
As he sat, wearing his kit.
But when he went on to the pitch,
It was obvious he wasn't fit.

The final group game was against Sweden,
Who England hadn't beaten for thirty-odd years.
In the first minute of play, Owen injured his knee,
Going off, he left the nation in tears.

Crouch came on as his substitute,
But, Sven hadn't many strikers to choose.
A win or a draw would do us fine,
But he knew we dare not lose.

Frank Lampard made several half-hearted tries,
But unfortunately his shots weren't true.
It looked as though the teams were evenly matched,
Until a chance came out of the blue.

In the thirty-fourth minute, the ball flew through the air,
And landed on the chest of Joe Cole.
He volleyed his shot, that arced quite high,
And went into the top of the goal.

Sweden equalised shortly into the second half,
When Marcus Allback pulled a goal back.
The two-thousandth goal in World Cup history,
For those that are keeping track.

Rooney started off full of running,
But by the seventieth minute, his pace had gone.
So he was taken out of the game,
And Steven Gerrard came on.

After a lot of frantic passing,
A cross came in from Joe Cole.
Gerrard headed in for a 2–1 lead,
With only five minutes to go.

England only had to keep the ball,
And, between them, keep on passing.
But in the final seconds, in front of goal,
Came a scramble, that let in Larsson.

The final whistle ended the game,
The result was a 2-2 draw.
Just enough for England to top their group,
And, in the next round, face Ecuador.

If they'd lost this game to Sweden,
They would have ended as runner-up.
And had to face host nation Germany,
In the next phase of this year's World Cup.

So, on they travelled to Stuttgart,
Now one of the last sixteen.
Fans throughout the country,
Ready to cheer on their team.

Sven made changes to their line up,
As they ran out onto the pitch.
This was now the knockout stages,
So he couldn't afford a slip.

Carrick was in the team for the first time,
With Rooney, the sole man up front.
He was backed up by Joe Cole and Gerrard,
As they went on an expected goal hunt.

The first half started well, with some nice little moves,
Then Ecuador shot, and hit the bar.
It frightened the life out of England,
Who looked average, and on a par.

The whistle blew at the end of the half,
As the score remained at 0-0.
The hottest day of the year, so far,
Was making the players feel ill.

The half-time talk must have had some effect,
Because it surely played its part.
For, when the teams came onto the pitch,
Their game improved right from the start.

Only a couple of minutes gone,
When England had a free kick.
The heat was still overpowering,
It made David Beckham quite sick.

He put his feeling to one side,
As the ball, he precisely placed.
About twenty-five yards away from goal,
while, in the box, the forwards all raced.

He ran, and kicked, with all his might,
And the ball soared into the air.
It ended up in the back of the net,
And left Ecuador in despair.

The team were elated and surrounded Beckham,
But he fell to his knees and threw up,
The heat had finally taken its toll,
In their quest to win the World Cup!

1-0 to England, and that's how it stayed,
Until the final whistle blew.
They'd beaten their opponents in the game,
And knew that they'd gone through.

Portugal beat Holland as well that day,
So, it would be them that England played next,
And, all thanks to that solitary goal,
Scored by their faithful skipper, Becks!

The roof was closed in Gelsenkirchen,
On the stadium, where the match was played.
The teams paraded onto the pitch,
Where statements against racism were made.

The play was very even,
Both sides failed to score.
The halfway finishing at 0-0,
It was getting to be a bore.

Gary Neville had played right from the start,
He fitted in, at the back.
Wayne Rooney, the single striker,
Sven's selection was taking some flak.

The second half had only just started,
When Beckham injured his foot.
He went off to get some treatment,
Things were not looking good.

He couldn't continue in the game,
So Lennon came on to have a go.
Then Rooney was shown the red card,
For England, a sickening blow.

Ninety minutes played, and still no score,
So extra time was beckoning.
Another fifteen minutes either way,
The ten men dare not let one in.

They couldn't break the deadlock,
The passion made fans feel sick.
It would now all be decided,
On their ability to take spot kicks.

The tension was increasing,
For the penalty shoot out.
As the teams linked arms, united,
In that, there was no doubt.

Portugal scored first, and the stadium erupted,
They'd found the back of the goal.
But Lampard failed to capitalise,
And England felt it in their soul.

A miss by the opposition,
Followed by a goal from Owen Hargreaves,
Gave English fans a bit of hope,
Amid ecstatic, jubilant scenes.

From that point on we failed to produce,
Gerrard and Carragher couldn't put it away.
Portugal scored a further two,
Ending England's World Cup day.

The players fell to their knees in despair,
They felt they'd given their all.
Exhausted, and totally devastated,
But they hadn't answered England's call.

Fans throughout the country,
Were seen crying, while trying to phone,
Consoling others, feeling their world had ended,
But the team was coming home.

I'm sure that any fan will tell you,
They didn't play their best,
But we owe thanks for the entertainment,
Now they can have a well earned rest.

Sven's last game in charge was not the result
That everyone wanted, and hoped.
His policies didn't materialise,
The team never really coped.

So, onto the next cup in four years time,
Steve McClaren will take control.
To bring youngsters to full potential,
The old faces, he'll need to console.

Beckham, resigned from the captaincy,
While holding back the tears.
He said that someone else should do it,
For the coming years.

Let's hope they find a strategy,
A plan to which England can play.
So, if we qualify for the next World Cup,
We'll all think, THIS could be our day!

NO WAY TO TREAT A CARROT

Pity the poor old carrot,
Planted as a minute seed;
Sun and rain to promote its growth,
Often mistaken for a weed.

Underground, its form gets bigger,
Above, it has a head of hair;
Flopping about, all over the place,
Drooping everywhere.

Then, when it's grown up, big and strong,
And has been duly fed;
Someone will grab it by its hair,
And pull it from its bed.

They'll scalp the little carrot,
And scrub its skin to get it clean;
Shove it in a basket,
Just like in a bad dream.

It'll go into a factory,
And be chopped in little bits;
Cubes, or rounded slices,
Or made into narrow strips.

Shoved into a polythene bag,
With a tie around its neck;
Then thrown into a freezer,
After a quality control check.

Later, in a cardboard box,
And sealed with sticky tape;
Transported in a lorry,
To a supermarket gate.

Again, into a cold room,
Along with all the rest;
Competing with all the others,
To see just who is best.

Taken to the brightly lit shop,
And stacked up on display;
When somebody comes to pick it up,
Sometime during the day.

It's thrown into a trolley,
And pushed around the store,
Along with other frozen bits,
Packets, tins, and more.

Slid along a conveyor belt,
And into a carrier bag;
The weight on top is tremendous,
The bag begins to sag.

Once home, again in a freezer,
It's no surprise it catches cold;
In and out so many times,
And still only a few days old.

Then, because somebody's feeling hungry,
It'll be tipped into a pot;
The water brought to boiling point,
With any other veg they've got.

When its body goes all soft,
It's slapped onto a plate;
Pierced with a fork; cut with a knife,
And that seals the carrot's fate.

Section 10

IT HAPPENED
TO MY COLLEAGUES

A DIY IN THE LIFE…

I was working at home the other day,
Making something out of wood.
I'd drawn my plan, and picked the grain,
Everything was looking good.

With safety in mind I donned my glasses,
Insulated on my rubber mat,
I wore my dust mask, ear plugs… and yes,
Even my safety hat.

I thought I'd got everything covered,
Kitted out from my head to my bum.
The only things I hadn't considered,
Was my fingers and my thumb.

I turned on the saw, it started to buzz,
And the rest I think you can guess!
The wood cut perfectly, just as it should,
But my thumb was a bloody mess.

It spurted and gushed from the open wound,
I caught most of it in a pail,
I looked on the floor, and sure enough,
There was half of my thumb and its nail.

Two weeks in August is just the job,
To recover from my ordeal.
I'll put my feet up and have a rest,
DIY has lost its appeal.

MICKEY AND AN OLD FLAME

Mickey Mulholland had a burning desire,
To get rid of his rubbish, so he lit a fire.

He piled it high, with the kindling set,
But it wouldn't light – the twigs were wet!

He scratched his head and he thought," I know,
I'll get some paper and have a go!"

But the paper was damp so he couldn't proceed
To dispose of the wood and the great pile of leaves.

He tapped his head and said, "Oh what a fool –
What this fire needs now is a dose of fuel"

So he looked around and he found a bucket,
With his Geordie accent he said, "Oh fook it!"

Mickey then said, "I do maintain,
That this fire will light with High Octane."

Not all from Newcastle are really this thick,
(but a boy scout can light a fire with a stick!)

Two gallons of petrol he put in the bucket,
And a box of Swan Vestas he put in his pocket.

Now, petrol and matches don't really mix,
But Mickey's aim was to get out of this fix.

He thought, "This bonfire will bloody light –
I don't care if it takes me half of the night."

He soaked the rubbish and wood piled high,
As he struck the match, flames shot to the sky!

Now, nobody knew of Mickey's plight,
But the neighbourhood said, "What a wonderful sight."

November 5th is a few weeks away,
But Mickey's bonfire has saved the day.

The sky lit up, but so did Mickey,
His situation was looking tricky.

The blast from the fire had sent him reeling,
The skin on his face and arms was peeling.

His eyebrows were singed and his face did burn,
But this Geordie lad will never learn.

The ambulance didn't take long to arrive,
But Mickey was lucky to still be alive.

Now he's back at work, his skin pinker than ever,
When asked if he'd learned his lesson, said, "Never!"

KAREN "SNOT" WELL

Vinny is suffering, 'cos Karen's not well,
He's having to do all the work!
He's run off his feet, the poor little chap,
He can't even find time to shirk.

Karen said she's got a bad migraine,
Lights flashing inside of her head.
It's spinning quite bad, and driving her mad,
She had to spend all day in bed.

Her vision was blurred this morning,
A cup of tea had no effect.
She couldn't see straight, so she said, "My mate
Vinny can cope, I expect."

"I'd better ring work," she thought to herself,
"Or I'll be in serious trouble."
So she phoned to say, "I'm quite ill today,
'Neath my bedclothes I'm having to huddle."

Her eyes were red where she'd rubbed them,
She wouldn't be able to drive.
Anyone with the luck to be in-front of her truck,
Would be lucky to walk away alive!

As we all know, our Karen has piercings,
And she's never been all that 'busty',
But the nose-rings she's got, are all full of snot,
And she fears that they might go rusty.

If Karen comes back tomorrow,
She'd better not spread her diseases,
With her coughs and cold, or so I'm told,
She's struggling to suppress her sneezes.

She's dosed up with Paracetamol,
She needs her chest rubbed with Vick,
But until she's well, you can call me Jim Bell,
Then I'm changing my name... (to Vic!)

IT'S A TO DO RON RON!

If ever you need first aid,
You can call on Ron Gillett.
He's had practice galore
With a doll on the floor,
(And, I've heard, with a girl called Bet!)

Well, I won't go into those details,
It's probably not true anyway,
So I'll tell of the story
That isn't so gory,
That will brighten up your day!

One day while on a first aid course,
Poor Ron had a little mishap.
The doll got a puncture,
So just at this juncture,
He thought, "I'm a lucky chap".

Mouth to mouth resuscitation was the plan,
But old Ron just couldn't cope.
As the doll went down on him,
He smiled, then started to grin,
From desperation was a sign of hope!

He found where the dummy was leaking,
And used his finger to try to plug it.
But the look on his face,
Was of total disgrace,
As he stood up in aroused discomfort!

He went very red in the face,
And the dummy just lay there deflated.
As he straightened his clothes,
From his head to his toes,
Ron was feeling very elated.

The other First Aiders attending the session,
Just didn't know where to look.
Should they whistle and clap?
To encourage this chap,
Or ignore him and study the book?

It's not every day you snog a model,
Of his achievement he was quite proud.
So he took a bow,
And that was how,
As the pain struck he cried out loud!

His back gave a funny clicking sound,
And he couldn't stand up straight.
He was frightened to move,
Even to prove,
That he could do it in-front of his mates.

The hour long course wasn't over,
So he had to read from the book.
He had to recite,
For the rest of the night,
Amid many a concerned look.

He's not able to work for a while, of course,
So he's resting at home on full pay.
With a puncture outfit,
He's ready to quit,
If his doll doesn't go "all the way!"

SOMETHING'S FISHY!

Dave has got a little 'un,
But he wants one three feet long,
'Cos when he's got a big one,
He knows he can't go wrong.

It gives him satisfaction,
When people stand and stare.
He judges their reaction,
When they say, "Well... that's not fair!"

They'd like one of proportions,
That are described by Dave.
But he tells them of precautions,
That they would have to take.

"You'd need to rest it on a stand
Because it gets quite heavy.
When you lift it, you need a hand.
It's really rather beefy!"

He started with a tiddly one,
It was very, very small.
It shimmered in the daylight sun
When the rays bounced off the wall.

He wanted to try his hand at mating,
So thought he'd better go to the shop.
There wasn't a queue waiting,
He was excited, and couldn't stop.

He told the man, who obviously worked there,
That he'd like another one,
So that he would have a lovely pair,
That could have some fishy fun!

I forgot to mention, it's a fish tank,
That Dave had as a Christmas gift.
He's really got his wife to thank,
But how do you wrap up a fish?

Once you get the bug for fish-keeping,
You want to buy more and more.
You look for the fish you are seeking,
In every aquatic store.

You get attracted by the colours,
As they swim around the tank.
But will they mix with the others?
How does their keeping rank?

A community tank is the best way to start,
You can get a nice collection,
Of guppies and platys and bleeding hearts,
Of gouramis there's quite a selection.

He will soon get the urge to expand,
Bigger tanks and a shopping list.
For the bits that you need to have on hand,
When you are an "Ichthyologist".

FIRE!

Keith just loves fire engines,
And all that they entail.
He can talk about them all day long,
Down to the last detail.

He'll tell the vehicles year and make,
And point out its equipment.
He'll describe its various uses,
In fire-fighting to an extent.

To me, a fire engine is red,
With a ladder on the top.
It comes when you ring 999,
A blazing inferno they can stop.

To Keith it means much more than that,
He can tell the full procedure
They follow when they answer calls,
Down to interviews with the media.

He's got books and pictures and trophies,
Of equipment and items of note,
That's been collected over many long years,
And he's got copies of letters he wrote.

He belongs to Firefighter's Societies,
And gets regular club bulletins.
He paints pictures on glass, and sells them,
To workmates, and members therein.

It's good to have a hobby,
In something you can believe.
In this case, it's fire engines,
So well done, and good luck Keith!!!

A TRUE STORY

The house on the hill was a daunting sight,
It was always dark – there was never a light.

They say the owner was tight with his money,
And it only looked good when the weather was sunny.

The family gathered all huddled together
For bodily warmth, whatever the weather.

His conscience was pricked so he opened his purse,
Out flew a moth – that made him curse.

He started to plan for a warm glowing house,
A place to return to children and spouse.

He went to Wickes but they looked at him queer,
He didn't know decimalisation was here.

He counted the pennies and white fivers also,
He'd got concealed on his warmly clad torso.

"This heating lark will take all my cash,
My DIY's good (?) so I'll have a bash."

He cut some twigs from the hedges and thicket
And took pallets from work (we hope with a ticket).

He couldn't use his saw for he was a finger short,
After a previous job that he had to abort.

With a hammer and nails he made a box,
It had a door at the front to take the logs.

Now, somebody should have told him sincere,
That a wooden fire's not a good idea.

But this intrepid old miser thought the project was good,
To burn his logs on a fire made from wood.

The family all gathered around the lit match,
To warm their hands on the glowing patch.

The fire did burn, and the orange flame
Did put this man and his DIY to shame.

The door caught fire, and the logs ablaze,
The warmth given out could only amaze.

The family's faces were all aglow,
But the extent of the fire they didn't know.

The fire brigade said that the house wasn't lost,
Insurance would pay when they worked out the cost.

The future looks brighter for the family enthralled,
As he pays for a fire and gets it installed.

You can't cut corners when buying a heater,
It'll be stronger than wood and will look a lot neater.

If you like, you can have one that hasn't a flue,
To bring heat and warmth to the family True.

BITS AND PIECES

Ian's got a collection,
Of cars and motorbikes.
He buys privately, and from auctions,
They're antiques, and the like.

Some are really tatty,
When he gets them home.
He knows they're never going to work,
So he strips them to the bone.

He gets down to the basics,
With piles of washers and screws,
With nuts and bolts that he's removed,
And bits he dare not lose.

When he's down to the chassis,
It gets a coat of paint or two.
Then he starts to build it up,
Replacing parts with new.

He'll send off for springs and gaskets,
And exhausts that fit the model.
Then he'll put it all together,
He thinks it is a doddle.

The money he spends on those spare bits,
And the paint, and grease, and oil.
He could have bought a new one,
And saved all the sweat and toil.

MRS MOP

Our cleaner in the morning,
Mops the rest room floor.
She also does the toilets,
And leaves her bucket by the door.

She never seems to smile much,
And doesn't have a lot to say.
I thought at first she was timid,
But she's like it every day.

One thing that I'd like to know,
When I want to go to the loo.
How does she always time it,
So she is in there too?

I try to make conversation with her,
As she sits in the canteen,
But all she ever seems to say, is
"Don't put money in that machine."

"Its swallowed up my pile of coins,
I fed into the slot.
I've got nothing out to show for it,
It's taken all the lot!"

Then, she puts her bucket in the cupboard,
And puts her mop away.
If you see her again the next morning,
She'll still have the same thing to say!

GOING DOWN UNDER

Two people at work took a welcomed break,
A much earned holiday.
They went to Oz,
Mainly because,
They had somewhere to stay.

He called her his Sheila,
While she renamed him Bruce.
They made this joke,
Til the poor bloke
Said, "Enough… lets call a truce!"

They visited sites of interest,
Did all the tourist things.
But in their travel,
Took time to unravel
The tale in the book, that he did bring.

He found he couldn't put it down,
So every chance he got,
He'd read some text,
Then turn to the next,
To get into the plot.

Unfortunately, she wasn't into books,
She wanted to relax.
She had a swim,
And looked at him,
Laying on his back.

He'd got his swimming trunks on,
A hat upon his head.
The corks did dangle,
At a funny angle,
As he lay upon the bed.

She was wearing her bikini,
Swimming up and down,
When she made a blunder,
And went under,
Trying not to drown.

He was oblivious to all of this,
About his story, he was starting to think.
With its Wizards and Ghouls,
While in the pool,
The poor woman was starting to sink.

He's always liked the idea
Of the supernatural, and stuff like that,
But he dropped his book,
As he dared to look,
At the sight of his wife in a flap.

She called his name when she came to the surface,
Blowing bubbles, and gasping for air.
He jumped to his feet,
And ran to meet,
The danger that was facing the pair.

He jumped into the water without thinking,
His hat flew off as he dived,
But he grabbed her arms,
(and ample charms),
and that's how his wife survived.

After a bit of choking and spluttering,
They managed to regain their pride.
They dried themselves off,
She continued to cough,
While their embarrassment they tried to hide.

A drink is what was needed,
So, to the bar they did go.
To have a lager,
Or if she'd rather,
A cocktail, or even Pernod.

It took a while to regain their composure,
But they have a tale to tell.
Was it just fate,
Or were they too late,
For the Wizard, who cast his spell?

They're back at work now after their rest,
To tell of where the pool is.
Of the trip down under,
And the poor woman's blunder,
And the book about his Ghoulies!

IT'S JUST A LITTLE PRICK!

Accidents that happen to people at work,
Can be accounted for, to the last man,
But at home you accept that things will go wrong,
So to that list you can now add Van.

Just like Richard and Mickey, that I've written of before,
David was the last to fall foul,
Of the DIY craze that's sweeping the land,
Now Van joins that list as well.

This man looks like Brutus in the Popeye films,
With his beard and his deep, gruff voice.
But in his bid to save a few quid,
Must now think that he made the wrong choice.

He wanted to work in the loft of his house,
So he put all of his tools in a box.
His fear was to slip, and put his foot through
The ceiling, so he took off his shoes and his socks.

He looked at the carpet he wanted to lay,
Then looked down at his ten bare toes,
He thought of the pain caused from carpet burns,
So put his socks back on... so the story goes.

Now, Van is anorexically challenged,
And the loft door was very small,
So he huffed and he puffed as he squeezed his bulk through
From the loft ladder that led from the hall.

As he struggled, he wobbled the ladder,
It dislodged the bits on the floor;
He peered from above, to see much needed parts,
So squeezed back through that tiny trap door.

The gripper rods used to lay carpets,
Are dangerous in the wrong hands,
So to a man who would jump with just socks on his feet,
It's important the way that he lands.

Van was never all that agile,
His movements slow…that's no exaggeration.
But the speed that he moved, when he jumped from the steps,
Left his feet with severe perforations.

He was impaled on the rods that were full of nails,
Both his feet were cut and bleeding,
He only wanted two more rods in his hands
And he'd look like he'd taken up skiing.

Never a man to be lost for words,
The air turned a deep shade of blue.
His wife heard him cry when he swore out loud,
There were some words she never knew!

He's been hobbling about in his office all day,
Walking like he's messed his nappy;
It's not wise to approach him when he's acting like this,
He doesn't look very happy.

Far be it for me to write a poem,
Making fun of this poor man's plight,
So I won't… I'll be good… and give it a miss,
I think that it's only right!!!

Van now joins that league of Indian men,
That lie on a bed of nails.
A "silly fakir", if ever I saw one,
Another DIY task that fails!

THAT SINKING FEELING

Poor old Mickey Mulholland,
Has never had very much luck.
First he tried self combustion,
Now he's swimming about like a duck!

I'll start at the very beginning,
His exploits to explain.
He was watching TV the other night,
When it suddenly started to rain.

It took a while for it to register,
Then he got that sudden feeling.
For what he thought was rain at first,
Was coming through the ceiling.

He rushed upstairs to find the fault,
It was a valve on the radiator.
He said "I'll try to stop it,
Or it'll be a problem later."

He was right you know, it did go wrong,
When he sat on the settee that night.
He tried to give his wife a cuddle,
But she had a terrible fright.

The ceiling came crashing around the pair,
The water did dampen his ardour,
He picked the wet plaster from off his wife,
And said, "We'll delay our snog, if you'd rather!"

She chose a few well used expletives,
To explain the way she was feeling.
As she looked at the bedroom radiator,
That was visible through the ceiling.

As they stared at the hole above them,
Their opinions were divided.
They wondered what their next step should be,
As the water level subsided.

They phoned the insurance company
Who seemed to think they ought to,
Change their home to a theme park,
'Cos it's already full of water.

It'll take time to put it straight again,
But I'm sure it will look much better.
If the job is done by a professional,
Our Mickey couldn't get any wetter!

HAYWARD'S PICKLE

David Hayward's a clever man,
Very competent and able,
Except when it comes to a project at home,
Constructing a wooden bird table.

He planned and made a pedestal,
But the house design left him muttering,
The mental anguish he suffered
Trying to decide on the type of guttering.

A bird-house that's built by David,
Could never be an eye-sore,
As he measured and trimmed the bits of wood,
He found that he needed his jigsaw.

He was working too far from a power point
To use the saw of his needs,
So instead of moving nearer,
He used a trailing lead.

He plugged in the saw and turned on the switch,
He turned, and was about to go,,
To the site of his wondrous construction:
He was focussed, and now in full flow!

With the saw in his hand he was taking great care,
Richard True had given him some tips
On Health and Safety while using power tools,
He didn't want to trip.

Trying to remember all he'd been told,
He returned to the towering bird table.
He was dazzled by its shear beauty,
As he got his foot caught in the cable.

He fell to the ground in a crumpled heap,
His work flashed before his eyes.
He reached for support to get to his feet
But that wasn't very wise.

He grabbed the table to pull himself up,
But gravity proved too strong,
It fell on top of the poor old chap,
Everything was going wrong.

His family rushed when they heard him call,
From beneath the pile of rubble.
They looked at dad, and the pile of wood,
And said, "That table's nothing but trouble."

From his hospital bed, David's voice can be heard,
When he recalls his narrow misses.
His saw and his table in countless bits,
A jigsaw of several pieces.

He suffered the pains of his efforts,
No one could call him a wimp,
But when he fell he hurt his leg,
And now he walks with a limp.

The birds don't need a table
That's strong, and sturdy and sound.
They certainly haven't got this one,
Let them eat from the bloody ground!

TROUBLED WATERS

Dave's fish just keep on dying,
And so he thought he oughta
Buy a kit from his local shop,
So he could test the water.

Some floated to the surface,
Others, they did sink;
He scratched his head to contemplate
And said, "Now let me think!"

Everything I buy don't last long,
It's dead when I get home.
Do you think I'm doing something wrong,
Or am I accident prone?"

He used to have a few fish,
He kept them in the hall.
Their tank was nicely heated,
But now he's got f*** all!

ENVIRONMENTAL MAINTENANCE OPERATIVE

Our cleaner's name is Cyril,
He wanders to and fro.
He nips into the offices,
You can spot him come and go!

He grabs the sack of rubbish,
And puts a new bag in.
It doesn't take him long at all,
To replenish your bin!

Sometimes you see him with a cloth,
Sometimes with a broom.
He flits about, just like a moth,
As he goes from room to room.

Occasionally, he gets his mop,
And sometimes gets it wet.
He dips it in his bucket,
He got them as a set!

He threatens the floor with water,
Sometimes, he makes it damp.
His mop is lacking dangly bits,
It's looking rather lank!

He's got a funny hairstyle,
Over his ears, it does flop.
I think it came originally,
From the design of his wet mop!

Although he gets on with his work,
He's got a heart of gold.
He tells me that he's twenty-one,
But looks ninety-nine years old.

He cycles here from his other job,
A cleaner at a school.
He fits it in throughout the term,
Arriving 1pm as a rule.

He talks about his leisure time,
When he uses his PS2,
He spends a lot of time on it,
Playing games… he's got a few.

I don't know what he's like at home,
Does he do the housework there?
His wife should get a GameBoy,
So Cyril can do his share!!!

'APPY TO HELP

Johnny Apps is our building contractor,
And he has a base on site.
He's got an office in the warehouse,
Where his desk is a terrible sight.

He's got papers, and things scattered everywhere,
Amongst pipes, and pots of paint.
A well paid job it may be,
But glamorous, it certainly aint.

When he wanders about, throughout the works,
He's often carrying a drill.
He'll make a hole in anything,
As long as it's standing still.

He's got a couple of ladders,
To reach jobs way up high.
'Cos he's only a little, short-arsed man,
almost miniature in size.

He chugs along on his dumper truck,
Carrying all the tools he needs,
To complete the job he's working on,
And satisfy everyone's pleads.

Sometimes, when standing in a hole,
You can only see his head and shoulders,
Sticking out above the mound of dirt,
And gravel, mud and boulders.

He'll always find time to chat a while,
After rectifying someone's mishaps.
If you've got a problem that needs sorting out,
You can rely on Johnny Apps.

MEL'S MONSTER

Mel was working in Assembly as usual today,
When she had a bit of a fright.
She felt something irritating on her leg,
But when she looked there was nothing in sight.

She continued working, but her discomfort got worse,
So she got help from her workmate, Mary.
When she looked at Melanie's trousers,
She saw this creature... quite big and hairy.

Mary was shocked – quite taken aback,
It was two inches long, or more.
She took a deep breath, and with all her might,
Knocked the monster onto the floor.

She jumped up and down on the helpless thing,
Mel was now in a state of distress.
The other women all examined their clothes,
In case they'd got something similar on their dress.

They scooped it up, and put it in a bag,
It had wings and a long stinging tail.
In the laboratory, it went under the microscope,
And Melanie went visibly pale.

The magnification showed it, for all it's worth,
As it lay there in all its glory.
Its body was bands of black and gold,
Where Mary'd jumped on it, it looked quite gory.

The veins in its wings looked fantastic,
It had a cluster of eggs, oozing out of its side.
But what was most astounding,
The bloody thing was still alive!

The insect was clearly moving,
As its body did pulse and beat.
Mary and Mel took another look,
Then blamed it on the heat.

"The hot weather must have something to do with it;
It's not the usual thing you'd see.
What would it do if it'd stung me?"
Came Melanie's frantic plea.

We reckon it could have proved fatal,
If Mary hadn't dived in to save,
Her from the sting of the monster.
She was incredibly brave.

The look on Mel's face at first though,
Was a sight to be seen for sure.
I'm certain that without the support of Mary,
She would have collapsed, and fell to the floor.

It finally stopped its moving.
No more wriggling of flesh and bones.
So, if either of them want to keep it,
They're welcome to take it home!!!

WHAT A SHOCK!

Production wanted to use Line 1,
In the Extrusion Factory.
So Greg was getting it ready to run,
When he received this plea.

Somebody shouted across the shop floor,
It was noisy… he had trouble hearing.
What it sounded like through the office door
Was, "Can you check the thermal steering?"

Always on hand to help his crew,
He jumped up straight away.
His men were busy – that he knew,
So he shouted back, "Yeah… OK".

The machine was heating up nicely,
The temps. were ready to start.
So Greg decided quite wisely,
To check out all of the parts.

He looked at the set conditions,
And checked all that he was able.
Then, by his own admission,
Grabbed hold of a power cable.

His hair stood on end as he started to shake,
The sparks around him flew.
He knew that he had made a mistake,
As he turned a nice shade of blue.

He was seen by some of the other men,
Twitching as he held the wire.
He was having a dance, it seemed to them,
Wriggling, like his arse was on fire.

They thought to themselves, "Well it's alright
For our shift leader to sing and dance,"
But if they had known, they'd have a fright,
He'd touched a live wire by chance.

Greg's hand was fused to the lead,
He found he couldn't let go.
He jolted and jerked and he pleaded,
As he shook from head to toe.

Somehow his grip relaxed its hold,
The cable fell from his smoking hand.
His body still jumped, or so I'm told,
When he touched a heater band.

He staggered to the office, to have a rest,
After his shocking ordeal.
He saw Richard True… he thought it best,
His hand was starting to peel.

Some bright sparks in the factory,
Made jokes of the poor man's plight.
But they asked if Greg was satisfactory,
He was a very sorry sight.

Hospital beckoned for this smoking chap,
Where they thoroughly checked him out.
As he told all he knew of his little mishap,
His shaking had another bout.

They decided he should stay for a night to see
If everything was OK,
They wired him up for an ECG,
In an observation bay.

They let him home the next morning,
His mum collected him when he phoned,
But all of a sudden, without warning,
He shut his eyes and just moaned.

His family and friends were very concerned,
As Greg looked a sorry soul.
He looked at his hand, as their comfort he spurned,
And all he could see was a hole.

When they phoned to see if he was feeling OK,
The company said with reluctance,
"We don't mind you testing… but do it the right way,
As long as we don't lose production!"

DECKING DUEL

Two men in Extrusion have waged a war,
About who could lay the best wooden floor.

The first one said his would shine, and gleam,
But the downside was, it was said by Rob Dean.

The second one said, "Let's make it the garden,"
So the challenge was being set by Dave Harden.

The outside version was the one they chose,
And the winner, would for a photo, pose.

Rob got some pallets, and lots of nails,
To hold them together, in case of gales.

Dave went to a DIY store for his bits,
And spent a small fortune on decking kits.

They both spent hours of toil on their task,
So that they could, for the photos, bask.

The pallets transformed Rob's garden just fine,
While he dreamed of sitting back, sipping cool wine.

Dave's kits were delivered, in flat pack style,
He checked it off, and stacked it in a pile.

Rob sanded and smoothed the wood with the grain,
Thinking of the bet that would be his gain.

Dave's pieces all clipped, and fitted together,
A master stroke, to combat the weather.

Rob's finished floor had a rail all around,
The boards were fixed, and it was nice and sound.

Dave had the advantage, buying it half done,

With the end in sight, he considered it won.

Rob's barrier was stained, and varnished and sealed,
With plants growing round it, the wood was concealed.

Dave finished his off with a nice wooden arch,
That led to the lawns, via a winding path.

Hanging baskets produced a floral display,
That both had tended for the judging day.

The deckings were set, with chairs and table,
They both had spent all that they were able.

A parasol shaded the eating venue,
And an outside heater was something new.

Rob stood back, and admired it all,
While Dave's thoughts were of having a ball.

They both had dreams of winning the bet,
With the prize going to the best deck yet.

They viewed their opponents, and liked what they saw,
So finally decided, that it should be a draw!

HARE TODAY...
(not gone tomorrow!)

"Quick lads," they shouted from their earth,
"Dig as fast as you can, for all you're worth."

Rabbits and hares all gathered round,
And started scratching at the ground.

They laughed and chuckled, full of mirth,
Saying, "Richard has just gone off to work."

The "Berlin Wall" that he'd installed,
Left the bunny population quite enthralled.

"He's tried his best, without a doubt,
But that fence of his won't keep us out!"

They dug down deep, with all they'd got,
And emerged the other side, in his vegetable plot.

They ate their fill from all he'd grown,
And made holes in his grass, all neatly mowed.

"When he gets home from work tonight,
He'll know he's got himself a fight."

"We'll leave a trail of destruction to show where we've been,
He won't get rid of us from his domestic scene!"

SHAKING ALL OVER

Mary, the secretary, moved to Hythe,
Preparing for her retirement day;
She'd used the money from the sale of her house,
So a mortgage she wouldn't pay.

Everything was going smoothly,
When she thought she'd take a trip,
To dispose of her old rubbish,
At the council's recycling tip.

Off she set, at 8 o'clock,
But as she drove along the road,
An alarm sounded inside her car,
She thought it must be her heavy load.

She ignored it, and kept driving,
Reversed up to the crusher,
Threw in her bags of debris,
With all the effort she could muster.

Suddenly, without warning,
The gantry began to shake;
A tremor spread throughout the site,
Leaving worried tippers in its wake.

It only lasted a couple of seconds,
She thought a blockage must be the fault;
So, off she drove to Tesco's,
There was shopping to be bought.

She was getting very low on fuel,
Would have to fill up, while she's out;
Didn't think that she would have enough,
Her return journey was in doubt.

She got to Tesco's car park,
Saw a crowd outside the door,
A suspected bomb in the Channel Tunnel,
Had forced evacuation from the store.

The management decided it was a false alarm,
And all were allowed back inside;
Staff restacked goods, fallen from shelves,
While security was strictly applied.

Only a short while later,
While Mary was still shopping, alas,
Once again there was evacuation,
Due to a very strong smell of gas.

Once her ordeal was over,
She drove, with her shopping, to the forecourt;
But as she approached the petrol pumps,
She had a sudden thought.

Would it be safe to top up her car,
With the smell of gas nearby?
She thought she'd better ask the question,
Rather than blow Tesco, and the garage, sky high.

Fortunately for them, they were on the ball,
And turned the pumps off… her heart sank;
It wasn't exactly her lucky day,
As she limped home with an empty tank.

At least she'd had some excitement,
Though, for a Saturday, it was quite scary;
But the only question we want to know is,
"Did the Earth move for you, Mary???"

FAMILY PLANNING

Just before Moulding started working four shifts,
The leaders were faced with over-manning.
So Caroline was moved from running her team,
To a place in Production Planning.

She plots the requirements of the warehouse,
By working out what products they need.
To replenish the mouldings that they have sold,
A request goes in… "Make this please!"

The quantity needs to be calculated,
What colours should be made, and when.
Will screws, or seals be needed?
Will they be cartoned in packs of ten?

She will need to make sure the material,
Is sufficient to meet her demands.
Labels and cartons must be available,
Machine capacity at her command.

Paul does the same job for Extrusion,
He plans how many pipes they need to make.
Which machines to run, and how they perform,
And how much material it will take.

They need the correct sized wood, for the bundles,
And sleeving for the products protection.
The suns rays can be very damaging,
All must be accounted for in his projection.

Paul and Caroline work together, like a family,
Their duties similar, in many ways.
They use the systems at their disposal,
To plan for the forthcoming days.

Extrusion production is gradually decreasing,
We don't make as much as we did in the past.
Moulding is still busy… but smaller,
So how long will any of our jobs last?

TROLLEY DOLLY

Look for a supermarket trolley,
Propelled by methods unseen.
Laden high with cups and syrups,
To top up the drinks machines.

It operates to a timetable,
More reliable than the trains.
Arriving on time every morning,
Whether sunshine, snow or rain.

If you delve beyond the piled high stock,
You'll see a lady, very keen.
She trundles along with the trolley,
She's short, and is called Maureen.

With her bucket and cloth she'll wipe inside
Each machine, where it gets sticky.
Sometimes she'll have a problem,
And can't get to a bit that's tricky.

Usually she keeps them running well,
We think she deserves an OBE,
But as that's out of our control,
She can help herself to a cup of tea!

ON THE EVE OF VALENTINE'S DAY

I overheard part of a conversation
By two ladies outside my door;
They'd stopped to have a little chat,
As they've done many times before.

One voice was raised, excitedly,
And although I'm going deaf,
I distinctly heard a person's name,
And "baby" mentioned in the same breath.

You don't need to be Hercule Poirot,
Columbo, or even Miss Marple.
All you need is a bit of gossip,
Spread by someone like Ena Sharples.

My imagination started working,
Putting together, two and two;
You can probably guess the outcome,
That's why I'm writing this to you.

Obviously, I can't congratulate you,
Or offer you words of praise,
Until the news is common knowledge,
And that won't be for several days.

You're going to make a smashing mum,
That is plain to tell;
So, for the lead-up to your momentous day,
I hope that all goes well.

THE SMELL OF FEAR!

As daylight broke over Gillingham,
In the rain, it was hard to tell;
But out of the gloom merged a figure,
In the shape of Ian Bell.

He met up with his mate, Jim,
Their bikes strapped to the back
Of their vehicles and their trailers,
They'd better be making tracks.

It was Sunday morning in Tenterden,
When they duly arrived.
They'd managed to get there in one piece,
It felt good to be alive.

They were both off-road virgins,
Facing a track for the very first time.
The rain had never stopped pouring,
The ground was just mud and slime.

Bikes unleashed from their anchorage,
They donned their riding suits.
Protective gear to keep them clean,
As they studied the "yellow" route.

The course led through trees and thicket,
Underfoot was mud and clay,
They could see in the distance, a stream
That seemed to be in the way.

This intrepid pair with racing gear,
Astride their shining machines;
White helmets, and goggles pulled in place,
Were as scared as they've ever been.

At the bottom of the hill were other bikers,
Modern machines, with riders old and young;
Jim and Ian approached on their Montesa's,
Old relics… out to have fun!

They approached the track without concern,
Keeping balance in the mud and rain.
Avoiding the ruts and puddles,
Trying not to think of the pain.

They twisted their way throughout the trees,
And came to the brow of a hill.
They halted to view the track ahead,
What they saw, made them feel ill!

The drop was about fifty feet or more,
Slippery chalk and leaves scattered the ground;
Ian's heart skipped a beat, Jim's belly jumped,
As the course ahead did astound.

Logs blocked the path about halfway down,
Beyond it remained unseen;
They knew they'd have to ride their luck,
And then on towards the stream.

You could almost hear their hearts pounding,
As they put their bikes into gear;
Ian was kind… he let Jim go first,
As he stood and watched in fear.

You could have walked faster than the speed he rode,
As he edged his way downhill;
Trying to keep the bike upright,
And avoiding having a spill.

He must have travelled about five yards,
Before the tyres lost their grip;
The bike drifted out from under him
And the whole thing started to slip.

He got to the bottom... just after the bike,
They both went their own separate ways;
Ian looked on at Jim's mishap,
From the top of the hill, in dismay.

"You silly fool", he called from above,
"I'll show you how it's done."
With true professionalism he started his ride,
And soon after slid onto his bum.

He followed Jim to the bottom,
Past the logs that had blocked their path;
This sorry pair looked at each other,
And both started to laugh.

No one was hurt they decided,
So remounted their bikes with pride;
Following the trail along the valley,
Their chugging machines, they were still astride.

A sharp left turn, then another,
Past a group of trees, and green;
They were faced with a hill going upwards,
The steepest they'd ever seen.

Ian managed to get his bike stuck in a ditch,
That ran just above the stream;
The heat was building, so he had to strip off,
As his body produced a cloud of steam.

Their clothing was out of the Fifties,
And they probably looked the part;
But their bodies would boil with exertion,
Somebody should have told them from the start.

They eventually reached their starting point,
Where they had tea and something to eat.
Then they took a good look at the woodland course,
Of this off-road trial bike meet.

After a couple of practice laps,
Their confidence grew and grew;
Watched by other bikers,
They looked professional, through and through.

They managed clear rounds of the circuit,
When somebody said, "If you like,
You can have a go on my machine,
It's a much more modern bike!"

The friendship offered by other participants,
Was welcomed, as was their support;
But Ian and Jim decided to stick
With the bikes that they had brought.

Everyone agreed that they'd done really well,
Participants, and even club members;
So they're planning their next session on the course,
For sometime in September.

A FANTASY

Vinny asked me to write a poem,
About Karen... to say something nice.
Well, I've given it a bit of thought,
And hope this will suffice.

When she appears, driving her fork-truck,
Silhouetted against the sun,
The rays highlight her flowing locks,
She's no longer the subject of fun.

She's always been good for a laugh and a joke,
Now she appears in a different light.
As a raving beauty with youth on her side,
Her character is an unblemished white.

She sets the men's pulses racing,
As she glides around on her truck.
Their hearts skip a beat when she approaches,
And they can't believe their luck.

She's the object of many fantasies,
And appears in lots of men's dreams.
As her mini-skirt shows her dark stockings,
And she stoops to straighten the seams.

I can't carry on writing much more of this,
It's making my pen start shaking.
It's too much to ask from a man of my age,
When Karen's there for the taking.

We must all try to get Karen out of our minds,
And let her get back to her roots.
For the girl that we all know, and love,
Is the one wearing hob-nail boots!!!

MEL, IN A NUTSHELL

A long time ago, a young girl arrived,
She was only in her teens;
Starting work in Assembly, at Key Terrain,
On a Youth Opportunity Scheme.

Harry and Jan, her parents,
Offered support in all she chose;
Her craving for pulsating fairground rides,
And watched her love of music grow.

As she's matured, she's developed a taste
For meals, consisting of several courses;
for spending time with her family and friends,
But her real love is for horses.

She'll spend her time grooming, and mucking out,
Wearing jeans, and a pair of green wellies;
But she'll have to stop when her baby's born,
And she gets rid of her bulbous belly!

Partner Craig, will change baby's nappy;
Mel will continue to fork the hay;
But today, of all days, we're thinking of her,
On this, her 40th birthday.

KEEPING HIS HAND IN

Robbie went to see his doctor,
Because he wasn't feeling well.
He knew he'd got a little pain,
But where, he could not tell.

He felt it when he walked,
And when he carried something heavy,
But it wasn't always there,
If he took it slow and steady.

Now, Robbie's always on the go,
He doesn't really stop.
He'll push to get the job done,
Until he's fit to drop.

The doctor took one look at him,
And said, "Cough, if you please.
I know I'm holding onto your balls,
But it's not meant to tease!"

He released his grip on Robbie's nuts,
And said, "I think I know
What's causing your little problem,
The pain is down below!"

"You get an intermittent pain,
But it's nothing to concern ya,
From all the prodding I've just done,
I can tell you've got a hernia!"

BY GEORGE!!!

Ian George came into work,
Though not feeling very well;
He was walking to the station,
On black ice, when he fell.

He was on a particularly nasty patch,
And that is when he slipped;
A double somersault and a single twist,
Followed by a backward flip.

Not wanting to lose his £100,
For attendance this coming year,
He continued to make his way into work,
While holding back a tear.

He didn't take his coat off,
When at the office, he arrived;
He started sorting through his papers,
His arm down by his side.

He still felt a little uncomfortable,
So when he rolled up his sleeve,
He saw a sight in front of him,
That is still difficult to believe.

His wrist was obviously broken,
Bones protruding in unusual places;
His shoulder joint was not quite right,
It turned out to be dislocated.

He asked for a lift to the hospital,
And somebody duly obliged;
Taking him to the outpatients,
Where they took him to one side.

First they repositioned his shoulder,
Then set about mending his wrist;
Sent him out with a plaster cast,
And, on a sling, they did insist.

He carried on working like a trouper,
His beard twitching at the pain;
How he cursed that patch of ice,
As he went to get his train.

Managing to finish his working day,
And making his way home;
He took his coat off in the evening,
And thought of his broken bone.

The swelling should have subsided by now,
Or so the doctor said;
But still his arm was painful,
As he got into his bed.

Next day, he noticed a fair sized lump,
And wondered what it could be;
So off he went to the hospital,
To let the doctors see.

They then made an announcement,
I guess it's their way of confessing;
For what was under Ian's skin
Was a piece of surgical dressing.

Poor old Ian, now it's been removed,
And his arm tends to no longer swell,
Can sit at his desk with his plaster cast signed,
And he has a good story to tell.

His little eyes glinting above his whiskers,
Peering across his desk;
Scribbling away at tremendous speed,
Putting his good arm to the test.

I know it's probably painful,
And difficult to deal with the staff,
Who work with him in the office block,
But you must admit... it gave us a laugh!!!

ENGLAND 4 – WEST GERMANY 2
(Mel's mum and dad – 1)

Mel, I was passing the time the other day,
When, suddenly, out of the blue,
An image appeared inside my mind,
That I need you to verify, if true.

Let me ask you a simple question,
Are your parents football fans?
Did they spend the summer of 1966,
Waving England scarves, and drinking beer from cans?

Or perhaps they thought the World Cup Finals,
When Hurst and Peters both managed to score,
Beating West Germany, by four goals to two,
Was nothing more than a bore.

My thoughts tell me that at half time,
When confidence in the team's ability grew,
Your mum and dad celebrated in their own way,
And nine months later, there was… YOU!

I've counted on my fingers,
And I think the sums do say,
That your parents enjoyed the extra time,
So for you, I wish a belated, Happy Birthday.

Section 11

PEOPLE POWER

SENTIMENTAL SOFTIE

Sometimes, I can watch a film,
Or programme on the telly.
When I feel a strange sensation,
A sort of tingling in my belly.

Depending on the subject,
About which the author wrote,
I get a tear form in my eye,
I get a lump in my throat.

I'm a sentimental softie,
That, I can't deny.
When something touches my emotions,
Tears stream down from my eyes.

I tell my wife I've got a cold,
As I try to wipe my face,
But those teardrops keep on forming,
As down my cheeks they race.

I don't know why it happens,
And it leaves me in confusion,
Sometimes, during TV programmes,
Showing family reunions.

I can't help the way I am,
My feelings, I must share.
I like to see a happy ending,
And I'd like to think, I care!

BRITISH PRIDE

Sunglasses perched on the end of your nose,
Your shirt opened to the waist,
From the end of your sandals peep your toes,
It's all in very poor taste.

Your belly balloons 'neath your great hairy chest,
Obscuring the top of your trunks.
You're feeling too hot so discarded your vest,
But you feel like a big, handsome hunk!

Your hanky is knotted, and sits on your head,
To protect you from the sun's rays.
On a deck chair, the beach, or even sun-bed
You'll spend your holidays.

You wanted an ice-cream; it dripped on your hand,
When you licked it, it went up your nose.
Your sandwiches really did taste of sand,
But that's the way it goes!

Each year we look forward to our holidays,
Abroad, we should fly the flag.
When in Rome, you follow the Roman ways,
Breathe in... lest your belly sags!

GOOD MORNING TV

Before I go to work in the mornings,
I switch on to GMTV.
It's not the news that I'm interested in,
It's the girls I like to see.

I always liked Jackie Brambles,
As she reported showbiz gossip a lot.
But now she's gone into semi-retirement,
(Has she had her screaming tot?)

It must be catching, this pregnancy lark,
It seems to come out of the blue.
I can't imagine just what causes it,
'Cos it happened to Kate Garraway too!

The lovely, blonde haired Amanda,
Always looks at her best.
As she reads her stories from auto-cue,
While seated at the news desk.

Cordelia seems to wander the streets,
Searching out stories, far and wide.
She's in a different location every day,
Nothing seems to put her off her stride.

Penny Smith was always my favourite,
She's lovely to look at, day or night,
But now she's facing a dilemma,
For John's attentions, she's got to fight.

He now shares the sofa with Gloria,
Who's the subject of many a man's dream.
But Penny's the one that I like the best,
Though, the competition is close, it would seem!

The weather is announced by Andrea,
So slimline, she always looks great.
She's bright and cheerful in the mornings,
And, on top of that, she's proved she can skate.

But the beauty of the set is Claire,
A gorgeous sight, in every way.
Her dark hair resting on her shoulders,
As she describes the weather expected today.

She always dresses so femininely,
With a blouse and skirt... or a dress.
For a poor old man ready to go to work,
She'll remove any signs of stress!

So GMTV, I thank you,
For starting my day off right.
I don't fancy John I can tell you,
But the girls are a gorgeous sight!!!!

A CLEAN START

The sudden shock of the water,
Concentrated into needle-like jets.
As it hits my skin,
Let my shower begin,
As I get myself thoroughly wet.

When I wash my hair with shampoo,
Water always runs into my eyes.
It makes me howl,
So I grab my towel,
That's the part of a shower I despise.

You can get a really good lather,
Shower gels seem to froth up, and stay.
As you wash your torso,
Arms and legs also,
And bits that don't see the light of day.

A good rinse, under running clear water,
To wash all the soap away;
Will make you feel better,
You won't get any wetter,
So you can start another new day.

A brisk rub with a clean, fluffy towel,
To dry all the bits on show.
Under your arms,
Not forgetting your palms,
Get dressed, then you're ready to go!!!

GOSSIP

When you've got a secret you cannot hide,
And it's eating away at your inside;
Avoid the people you can't abide,
And decide on the one in whom to confide.

Unleash your burden, with no holds barred,
Catching the listener completely off guard;
Reveal the gossip on the one you've tarred,
Leaving their reputation scarred.

Of course, there may be no truth in what you say,
You overheard it in conversation the other day;
Now it's out of your hands, and on its way,
Spreading like wild-fire; someone's going to pay!

IT'S YOUR PARTY

It's your birthday, and you're having a party,
You've spent all day blowing up balloons;
There'll be sandwiches and cakes and crisps and things,
Your friends will be arriving soon.

The table is set with a table cloth,
Birthday confetti in tinfoil strips;
Streamers ready to be thrown at will,
In the fridge there are instant whips.

There's jelly to be had at some point,
A cake, iced with your age and name;
Cards displayed on the mantle-piece,
You're ready for fun and games.

The doorbell rings… you run to the door,
There's a brightly wrapped gift thrust forward;
Your face is beaming, from ear to ear,
As you receive this birthday award.

Eagerly ripping the paper away,
You discover what's hidden within;
Drop the parcel, and rush once more,
As the doorbell again does ring.

Collecting cards and gifts by the handful,
You put them onto a chair;
There's lots of noise and excitement,
Music starts playing somewhere.

After tea you play Pass the Parcel,
All seated on the floor;
The package going round and round,
The music stops… remove one layer more.

Later, a game of musical chairs,
Your friends all want to win;
But as this is YOUR birthday,
Their chances are very slim.

You chase up and down the garden path,
With your friends all in tow;
Soon the party will be over,
It'll be time for them to go.

They put on their coats, and you say, "Goodbye,"
As you see them out of the door;
But don't you think you're a bit old for this,,
Now that you're forty-four?

GIRL WATCH

Seated in the park, watching girls go by,
He takes a deep breath, then gives a sigh.
The hottest day of the Summer yet,
He imagines the girls, with their shirts dripping wet.

The tight, hugging tops, that are cropped quite short,
Worn fashionably with the skirt they've just bought.
He ogles their breasts, just ripe to squeeze,
Then looks at their mum's... dangling by her knees.

The hems of the skirts barely cover the bum,
He admires the sight... it's a lot of fun.
A connoisseur of the female form,
It'd attracted him from the day he was born.

Since the day his mum, with her breasts hanging "south",
Shoved a teat into his mouth.
No matter how he tried, there was no concealing,
The way he was, and his funny feelings.

Another girl passed, wearing least by far,
He observed that she wasn't wearing a bra.
He shuffled, uncomfortably, on the bench,
Moving on for him, would be a wrench.

The constable travels this path each day,
Otherwise, this is where he would stay.
He's admired the scene, and all on show,
So now he thinks it's time to go.

POOR ME

I've got a headache, I think it's the heat,
It's making my eyes quite runny.
From the top of my head to the tips of my feet
I shiver; and even my tummy
Feels awful, although I've eaten quite well,
I'm sure I've picked up a bug or two;
I've not been sick, but I'm feeling quite ill,
Do you think it could be the flu?

If I feel like this in the Summer spell,
How will I be when the weather gets colder?
I'll wrap up warm, and aim to keep well,
Until I'm feeling much bolder,
To face the world with a spring in my step,
And to say, "I'm feeling fine."
With vim and vigour, and full of pep;
Well I think it's about bloody time!

A CHOICE CUT OF MEAT

Brenda works in Sainsbury's,
Where she spends all day on the deli,
Preparing all the goodies,
To fill the most hungry belly.

One day, while topping up the trays,
(At this time of year – that's no mean feat!)
Somebody asked her if she could slice
A bit more of their favourite meat.

Always ready to oblige,
And facing an ever growing queue,
She grabbed her knife to open a pack,
And that's when the air turned blue.

Fancy putting your finger under the blade,
Just to see if it really cut well!
It did… and that's when she realised,
She'd been a silly girl.

Blood spurted and gushed from the open wound,
So she grabbed at a wad of tissue;
She managed to contain the constant flow,
But that wasn't the main issue!

The lady at the counter who asked for the meat,
Said, "I don't think that's really fair,
When I asked for the beef, I wanted it red,
But your blood has gone everywhere."

"Thank you madam," said Brenda,
Polite, right to the last;
Only when she turned away
She shouted out, "Damn and blast!"

The walls and counter were crimson,
Blood spots covered all of the meat;
No longer suitable for human consumption,
Food nobody would want to eat.

At hospital, they stitched her together,
Her finger bandaged, she shed a tear,
They said she shouldn't return to work,
Until early in the New Year.

So, over Christmas you'll find the family,
Gathered round the kitchen sink;
Washing blood off slices of topside,
And the ham, that's already pink.

We hope you get better, Brenda,
Put your feet up, and have a rest;
When your finger stops its throbbing,
You can put it to the test.

You can use it to summon a supply of food,
And drink…because you're not well;
Disguise the fact that you can get about,
Say you're ill… no one can tell!

Make the most of this extra break,
Get your finger back feeling strong;
'Cos Christmas is almost upon us,
And the New Year won't be long.

IT'S A SNIP

She'd just been to the hairdressers,
I'd stood outside for an hour;
When she went in, she had dark hair,
Now, it looked like it was sprinkled with flour.

She said she wanted it coloured,
And could see nothing wrong;
I said the choice was up to her,
So I went along.

She felt she was getting very staid,
Almost stuck in a rut;
So, she booked up to get highlights,
A blow dry, and a cut.

After washing and drying her shoulder length hair,
Head held backwards, over basin and tap;
She was transformed into Yul Bryner,
Fitted with a perforated, rubber cap.

Strands of hair were pulled through the tiny holes,
And the colourant put on;
All this time I'm pacing up and down outside,
It's like a marathon.

The cap removed, and the light coloured hair
Contrasts well with her darker head;
Then snip, snip, snip with the scissors,
As, over off-cuts of hair, the girl did tread.

Combed and brushed into her usual style,
Everything sprayed into place;
Her new appearance, I must admit, looked quite nice,
Accentuating her pretty face.

PUBERTY

Puberty arrives and
Exams are looming;
Starts taking pride
In personal grooming.

Boys start calling
On the telephone;
And after school
Walk her home.

Mobile phones are
The latest gear;
Seemingly glued
To her ear.

Music blaring
From her speakers;
Room vibrating
From woofers and tweeters.

Friends calling round
All hours of the day;
Not afraid to speak up,
And have her say.

Teenage jibes
At mum and dad;
But she's a lovely girl,
Not really bad!

RED NOSE DAY

Shoes… wet from the frosty grass,
As I shuffle across the heath;
Foliage, now emphasised in white,
Covering the greenery beneath.

The magnificence of cobwebs, finely spun,
Their intricacies clearly defined;
A lone spider residing amongst the dew,
Its beauty, much maligned.

Clouds of steam, as I regularly exhale,
Form from breath in-front of my face;
Then disperses in the crisp, cold air,
To be lost without a trace.

A stamp of foot, and clap of hands,
Rekindles my appreciation of body heat;
A stroll on a morning, such as this
Is a luxury, that just can't be beat.

Admiration of Mother Nature's winter coat,
When all around takes a pallid appearance;
Too soon will return the warmer days,
That I endure with perseverance.

Not everybody waits for long, hot days,
To strip down to very few clothes;
For me, I prefer the winter months,
With rosy cheeks, and a bright red nose!

AT LAST!

After a lot of grunting and groaning,
And sweating, getting into a lather,
The job was finally successful,
I was told, "You're going to be a father."

Well, they say that practice makes perfect,
And the practice was a lot of fun,
We'd achieved what we'd always hoped for,
We now had a baby son!

In this life you get what you work for,
You set targets, achieve them, and later
Reset them for future ambition.
To eventually produce a daughter.

All that effort paid off in the end though,
Our daughter now plays with her toys.
In this life you get what you work for,
A girl amongst fourteen boys!!!!

BROKEN DREAMS

It's dark outside and I'm huddled beneath
The duvet, where I'm having a dream.
My sleep is shattered by the buzz of the clock,
Time to get up... or so it would seem.

As I reach from beneath the bedclothes,
I grope for that damned alarm,
That's insisting that I get out of bed,
And disturbing my nocturnal calm.

I find the button to stop the noise,
That emanates from the timepiece.
I open one eye and peer into the dark,
Peace again, now the buzzing has ceased.

I know I can't lay here, I've got to get up;
Got to go to work for sure.
So I gently pull back the bedclothes,
And put one foot onto the floor.

It's cold, and it's dark, and miserable,
I don't want to get up today.
So I put the other foot onto the floor,
Wishing that I could stay.

My other eye is now opening,
My hair stands on end, and goes its own way,
But just as my body prepares me for work,
I think, "Hold on... it's Saturday!"

I can stay in bed a while longer,
No need to get up so soon.
I'll jump back under the covers,
And sleep until it's noon.

But now it's getting light outside,
I wonder how long it will take,
For me to go back to sleep again,
Now that I'm wide awake!

EVERY PLACE HAS GOT ONE

Why don't people mind their own business?
Always putting obstructions in the way,
Butting into conversations,
Feeling they must have their say.

Every work location has got someone,
Who's always gone one better,
They think they're always ahead of you,
In their mind, they're a real "go-getter!"

If you said in a guarded moment,
That you'd built a six feet high wall,
They'd announce that their's was bigger,
Standing eight feet tall.

You may talk of going on holiday,
To the other side of the world;
Then up they'd pipe with their version of events,
Of how their round the world trip unfurled.

If your garden was measured at sixty feet long,
Their's would be double that,
But if you think of it in realistic terms,
They probably live in a flat.

These people really are a pain in the arse,
Thinking they know all there is to know;
For ever sticking their oar in,
Never knowing when to go.

Their opinion is always the best there is,
Certainly better than any you've got;
Never hesitant in coming forward,
Throwing their comments into the pot!

If only they'd get on with their job,
Instead of sticking their nose into mine,
Then a lot more output would be achieved,
And we'd probably get on just fine.

But no...they want to be nosy,
About things that are not their concern;
Why can't they mind their own business?
Will they never learn?

IMMIGRANT WORKERS

Just look at England's hospitals,
Where you go to be cured of your ills;
They're full of foreign doctors,
Practising their skills.

You can't go far without seeing,
A face from an ethnic caste;
Nurses and attendants,
Getting you processed, fast.

If you go out for an evening meal,
Your loved one to impress,
Chances are you'll be served by someone
Wearing evening dress.

But when you give him your request,
After you have made your choice,
He'll confirm it from his order pad
In a foreign voice.

When you get a takeaway,
To have your meal at home,
You only have to select your needs,
Then pick up the telephone.

Your preference may be Chinese,
Or perhaps, an Indian curry;
Pizza's delivered by a man on a moped,
Getting it to you in a hurry.

There's people of all nationalities,
Whose work we can't do without;
Contributing to the country's welfare,
Of that, there's little doubt.

We're expecting an influx of people,
From Romania, Bulgaria and Poland;
Hoping for a better life,
Than they had in their homeland.

The wages here do far exceed,
Tenfold, what they currently get;
So they're prepared to do menial tasks,
On that you can surely bet.

In this Country, our home grown youngsters,
Are brought up with all they need.
They don't have to scrimp and scrape for much,
Their families to feed.

The State will always help them out,
There's no need to do low paid work;
Let somebody else get dirty,
Sit back and collect your perks.

So, thanks to the foreign workers,
Always prepared to work flat out;
Not frightened of a long day's graft,
Money's what it's all about.

The new batches of immigrants,
When they land on our shore,
Will fit into the community,
Just like they've done before.

A SCREW LOOSE

I've only got one pair of glasses,
But I really should buy more;
The other day, I had an accident,
The little screw dropped on the floor.

I searched around on hands and knees,
Having to rely on touch;
Found it in the pile of the carpet,
It hadn't bounced that much.

My heart jumped, as I picked it up,
Between finger and thumb it was gripped;
So pleased that I'd actually found it,
Where, from my spectacle frames, it had slipped.

I put it in the palm of my hand,
I couldn't focus, it was all blurred;
I needed to hold it six feet away,
But that was quite absurd.

I couldn't line up the arm with my glasses,
The hole was so very small;
No matter how much I tried it,
I couldn't do it at all.

I'd need my glasses to see the hole,
But it was my glasses that were broke;
I couldn't put them onto do the repair,
It was getting beyond a joke.

When I took them off, I couldn't see a thing,
I screwed up my eyes, and tried to stare;
The only answer to my problem was
To buy another pair!

SAY IT WITH FLOWERS

When you think that you're in love,
You will tell the girl in question,
Anything she wants to hear,
Just to make a good impression.

You can tell her anything,
Be it the truth, or a pack of lies,
But if she ever finds you out,
It's YOU that she'll despise.

A box of chocolates keeps her sweet
With its hard centres and creams.
That should keep you in her good books,
And constantly in her dreams.

Perfume will add an aroma,
That will certainly make her smell nice.
Before you tell her there's an improvement,
You had better think twice.

If she now smells better,
You'll need to have an excuse;
Because that implies she's usually worse than that,
So she'll bombard you with abuse.

Most ladies like a bunch of flowers,
In multi-coloured blooms.
To brighten up their dullest days
And lift them from their gloom.

Beware though, before you push your luck,
And try to tease or squeeze her.
For all you know, it may not work,
She could suffer from hayfever!

TWO FACED

People have funny faces,
Their attributes can be extreme.
Not many features are similar,
Quite different, in fact, it would seem.

There's dainty, little turned up noses,
And heads that are covered in curls.
Lips that are full and pouting,
On young, good looking girls.

Some chins are full of whiskers,
Usually found on trendy men.
But sometimes found on women,
If they're let out, now and then!

Some ladies plaster on make-up,
They use a trowel to make it stick.
A confidence booster in their minds,
But to men... it makes us sick.

Faces can be fat and rosy,
While others are skinny and white.
Noses can be stumpy, or broken,
But some can glow in the night.

It's good that we're all different,
It wouldn't be fun if we were the same.
Wouldn't it be awkward to distinguish,
In times of trouble, which one to blame!

BREAK THE CHAIN

You don't need to be so bad,
To challenge every law;
Thousands like you have tried it,
Many times before.

Why try to rock the system?
Why break all of the rules?
Put in place to prevent society,
From thugs and mindless fools.

You tell your tales of boredom,
Of nowhere for you to go;
So you hang around street corners,
Walking, to and fro.

Because you're chilly, you wear hoodies,
To keep your ears nice and warm;
But hang about with all your mates,
Refusing to conform.

There's no excuse for graffiti,
Covering everything in your wake;
Can't you see it ruins the community?
Wake up – for Heavens sake!

Why steal from other people?
Who work hard for all they've got.
You think that if you rob them,
You can take the bloody lot.

Cars and property vandalised,
By gangs of marauding youths,
Spoiling life for everybody else,
Need to hear a few home truths.

You too, one day, will be older,
And have property to call home;
Something that you're proud of,
Something all your own.

A car that you do cherish,
Polished, shining bright;
So, how do you think you'd feel,
If it was damaged in the night?

And what about your children?
Do you want their lives the same?
Growing up in violent precincts,
Daughters going on the game.

Why not put that misspent energy
Into doing something worthwhile?
Change from an idle layabout,
Into someone much less vile.

There's a lot of organisations
That will get you off the street;
Local halls and community centres,
Places where you all can meet.

Alone, you make little impact,
In anything you do;
But enrol your mates, and together
You can see it through.

There may be no reward, financially,
But what do you get from standing around?
You need to break that vicious circle,
And find some common ground.

If your heart is in the right place,
(And I'm sure most peoples are,)
Approach life with a smile,
Greet people, near and from afar.

Help out by clearing rubbish,
Put it in a black sack;
Once the community spirit gets you,
There'll be no looking back.

Clean writing from the city walls,
Encourage others not to do wrong;
Try to convince your wayward pals,
Get them to tag along.

Youth groups encourage youngsters,
To give them a sense of purpose;
Nobody in this big, wide world,
Is absolutely worthless.

You can personally add a value,
To anything you care to do;
Break away from all the hangers-on,
There's opportunity waiting for you.

Don't ever think you're at a dead end,
With no one to turn to… to ask,
The only thing required of you,
Is take on a simple task.

Put your energy into a project,
You choose… there's lots to do;
Make something out of your young life,
Stick with it, and see it through.

Six months from now, you'll wonder,
Why people write on walls;
Loiter in shop doorways,
All without a cause.

You'll have somewhere to go each day,
A task for you to achieve;
With help and advice to guide you,
From others, who are born to lead.

Go on… make a difference!
Help your area… tell your mates;
For getting involved in local projects,
It's never going to be too late.

You'll have somewhere to be proud of,
Where your kids can feel safe to walk;
Don't let them go down that same old route,
Sit them down, and have a talk.

Use your story as a parable,
When you had nothing useful to do;
Tell how you avoided trouble,
Bring them up to be proud of you.

THE PARTY PIECE

Do you remember the office party?
Just try – see if you can.
The way you chatted to people,
Especially every single man.

You staggered your way through the evening,
A glass permanently in your hand;
Bashing into other revellers,
It was all you could do to stand.

I bet you don't recall the moment,
When Ada in sales did a striptease.
And when she took her bra off,
Her tits dangled round her knees.

And what about old Gladys?
You know – her that's in accounts,
Putting away all that whiskey,
In such vast amounts.

Some of the men were no better,
Shouting and swearing til the air was blue;
Making approaches to all the girls,
Then trying their luck with you.

The stationery cupboard seemed permanently locked,
From the inside… I wonder why;
But later in the evening,
You were wearing a man's tie.

And why did you have your knickers,
Thrown around the floor?
Was it really necessary
To say you wanted more?

I wonder if you'll still be here,
About nine months from now;
You'll never remember the father's name,
You dirty little cow.

But I suppose, just after Christmas,
After careful negotiation,
You will be the next in line
For automatic promotion.

I remember seeing the manager,
His shirt was all undone;
Coming from the cupboard,
After he'd had his fun.

You staggered out shortly after,
Tinsel in your hair;
Trying to look casual,
You didn't even care.

No, I bet the party's just a blur,
Detached from your mind;
I've heard about these goings on,
And people of your kind.

I suppose I'm jealous really,
For I had to drive my car;
I couldn't even have a drink,
And was the soberest there, by far.

You certainly know how to put some away,
And, in my mind I'll remember it well;
But your antics will be my secret,
I promise I'll never tell!

BELIEVE IT OR NOT

Imagine, a party conference,
In a hypothetical situation;
Where the leader of the government
Was talking to the nation.

He'd announced he would be leaving,
Said he'd be standing down;
Then, up popped a man to take his place…
Let's call him Mr. Brown.

Now, Mr. Brown didn't always get along
With the man he hoped to replace;
They'd had many public arguments,
Often, face to face.

Although the PM still had control
His party said he should leave;
Now that he'd announced his intentions,
To linger, was hard to conceive.

Mr. Brown had visions of power in his mind,
So, when he made his speech,
He told of the little disagreements,
Over problems out of their reach.

He claimed that he'd always liked the leader,
And (not like the media did send),
They always got on very well,
In fact, they were the best of friends.

A lady's voice came out of the blue,
Wearing a grey wig and long black smock;
She shouted out, in great concern,
"That's a load of complete bollocks!"

"You never liked him in all the time,
That he has been in power;
Now I stand here, listening to all you spout,
Lie after lie; hour after hour."

This fictitious barrister defended him to the end,
Nothing said by Mr. Brown,
Would have an effect on her opinion,
Nothing could calm her down.

Outside, when the meeting was over,
The nation's press met her, face to face;
And asked why she said the things she did,
She denied it had taken place.

She refused to admit to any wrong-doing,
And said, "I must conclude,
That everything stated in the press,
Has been totally misconstrued."

Well, thank God this story's fictitious,
Because people have a right to say,
Anything that they are feeling,
And you can't run a Government this way!!!

THE LONG WAIT

I give a big sigh, and look at the clock,
The fact that I'm here is a sign.
All this waiting about is killing me,
Why can't others be on time.

I uncross my legs, then walk the room,
My watch gets another glance.
You'd think they'd make an effort,
I've given them every chance.

I sit and try to concentrate,
I tap my fingers to a tune in my head.
But all the time, I'm ill at ease,
Waiting for them instead.

Once again, I pace up and down,
Will they never arrive?
Tut-tutting out loud, as I stare at the time,
It's already seven thirty-five.

The programme is certain to start quite prompt,
It's scheduled to begin at eight.
So why can't others be here on time?
I'm sure we're going to be late!

LADIES OF THE NIGHT

On Sunday nights I park my car,
While I complete my time sheets.
Beneath the glow of the lamp light,
Partially illuminating the streets.

From the shadows stepped a figure,
Seen from the corner of my eye;
It's difficult to keep writing,
But I knew I'd have to try.

As the girl approached my car,
She was quite an ugly sight;
It crossed my mind that she must be,
A Lady of the Night.

She must have been about thirty five,
Black boots up to her knees,
Her skirt was like an extra wide belt,
In her attempts to please.

Her face was plastered with make-up,
As she stooped to look through the glass,
Her hair was lank and greasy,
As her skirt rode up her arse.

I looked up from my paperwork,
And the sight was rather shocking;
I automatically reached for the door,
And applied the central locking.

A wave of the hand to indicate,
That I'm not there for her trade;
Not interested in what she's selling,
Or any offers made.

She strolled slowly along the footpath,
Trying to attract the men;
Cars pulled into the roadside,
Then drove away again.

Other girls regularly work the streets,
In this part of the town;
They can be seen almost any night,
Walking up and down.

Some are quite attractive,
And most are very young;
Trying to pick up passing men,
For their bit of fun.

Occasionally a car will stop,
And the girl will get straight in;
Off they drive, presumably,
To spend an hour of sin.

The risk must be tremendous,
As they don't know what they'll face;
When the driver lets them out of the car,
In some deserted place.

I'm sure my observations
Will keep me fully equipped,
With information for my poems,
But I'm keeping my trousers zipped!

DON'T CHANGE

Please, don't ever change,
I like you just the way you are.
You'd stand out in any crowd,
The best looking girl by far.

Your hair is long, and silky,
And reaches to your shoulders.
You've got that timid little smile,
That sexy look that smoulders.

Your body's tall and slender,
With curves in just the right places.
When you're walking down the street,
You should see the look on men's faces.

You've got a little, turned up nose,
And lips that look so pure.
If I was ever feeling ill,
You'd be the perfect cure.

You're voice is slightly husky,
When you laugh, it's just a giggle.
When I see you walk away,
I admire your bottom's wiggle.

So, please don't change the things you've got,
They're lovely to admire.
I'm only human, after all,
And you set my heart on fire!!!

THAT SPECIAL PLACE

They strolled hand in hand,
Along the sandy bay,
As the sunlight faded
At the end of the day.

It was three years ago,
When first they met,
When encouraged by his friends
He approached her for a bet.

But the laugh was on them,
Beneath those azure skies,
As he tentatively stared,
Into her beautiful eyes.

He was captivated by her features,
And her body, tanned,
As he introduced himself,
And shook her by the hand.

They chatted a while,
Then he gave her a wink,
And with all of his charm,
Asked if she'd like a drink.

While out together,
They seemed a perfect pair;
As he paid her compliments,
And stroked her hair.

They made each other laugh,
Her eyes formed a tear,
They pledged to return to this spot,
Same time, every year.

And, so it was,
They now walked in the sand,
Still madly in love,
As he held her hand.

They strolled along the water's edge,
As the ripples lapped the shore,
The evening silhouettes against distant lights,
Just like all those years before.

The humid evening, warm on their skin,
They stopped at a pre-determined place.
He turned towards his one true love,
And gently kissed her on the face.

Their spot… where they first shared a kiss,
Like birds, they returned each year.
Revisiting, to relive their fairy tale,
Remembering that first, joyous tear.

Next year, when they return again,
To paddle in the sea,
There'll be a noticeable difference,
For then they will be three.

Their first child due in three months time,
Will be their special guest;
Cementing their relationship,
And making it truly blessed.

They'll tell their story in years to come,
Of the place where their love grew.
With their child now part of their union,
Returning to that spot, under skies of blue.

Section 12

WHO CARES?

WHO CARES?

My full time job is with Terrain,
Although my time I like to share,
With my part time work at weekends,
For a company called London Care.

They supply carers to look after old folk,
In their own homes they do dwell.
Sometimes they've been in hospital,
So we tend to them as well.

I joined the company six years ago,
The people I work with are great.
We meet such marvellous people,
Who just want to communicate.

Sometimes they want to talk a while,
And have a cup of tea,
It's conversation that they're lacking,
So they can talk to me.

Often they need to take medication,
So we prompt them when we call.
We cook their meals when needed,
We care for them, one and all.

With age comes many problems,
Dementia, Alzheimers and stroke,
Heart problems, arthritis and frailty,
Their situation is no joke.

They could find it difficult to walk,
To sit, to stand, or move.
We offer support to live their own life;
They must have the right to choose.

Sometimes their health is poorly,
And they cannot get out of bed.
They suffer from incontinence,
So have a catheter fitted instead.

We empty out their night-bags,
And give them a bed bath.
They're human beings after all,
So I try to make them laugh.

The commode needs cleaning out,
But we do it with a smile,
Some people squirm at wiping bums,
We do it all the while.

Occasionally we need to use a hoist,
To lift people from their beds.
Two carers are needed to do this task,
So we don't drop them on their heads!

The clients welfare is a priority,
Confidentiality is a must.
No gossip, no spreading of rumours,
They must have the carer's trust.

Unfortunately, with age comes illness,
One day we will all meet an end.
So the news that someone you've cared for
Has passed on, means you've lost a friend.

If you're going to be a carer,
You need the right sort of approach,
You need to think about others,
But on their privacy must not encroach.

The training for this job is ongoing,
To meet the needs of me and you,
To obtain the qualifications,
In the form of an NVQ.

The course I've done is now finished,
It's in "Health and Social Care",
I feel better now it's completed,
So my new found skills I can share.

If you are interested in looking after others,
Whose misfortune is to age or fall ill,
I recommend the job as a carer
It's not just "run of the mill"!

You'll face many daily challenges,
But the friends you make will ensure,
That you fulfil your duties to such an extent,
That you'll want to come back for more.

It's got to be a job in a million,
I'm sure nothing can compare.
To the satisfaction you have of a job well done,
When you're working for London Care!

MY FINAL BREATH

I lie on the road in a pool of blood,
Not a movement from body or limb;
My clothes are torn, and my life is wrecked,
But my mind is still active within.

Broken bones, splintered from the sudden impact,
As the speeding car lost control;
It mounted the pavement, and hit with such force,
That's the last thing that I know.

The pain's taken over my body,
My head's filled with pulsing sounds;
I am wet, where my blood flows freely,
Broken glass litters the ground.

My life ebbs away, still wracked with pain,
Family and friends, fleetingly pass through my mind;
Brief glimpses, the last I'll ever see,
Of those that I'll leave behind.

Distant sirens are screeching, but they're too late,
To piece together my shattered shell;
I'll die without dignity, on this lonely road,
Close to the spot where I fell.

My children will cry, and my wife will weep,
The local community will stop, and think;
They'll erect a sign warning motorists,
Of the dangers of driving, and drink.

That won't help my family, though,
A bucket of sand will soak up my blood;
I'll be taken from the scene in a black-zipped bag,
Away from the people that I love.

ELDERLY ABUSE

Who'd want to abuse the old folk?
They're somebody's parents, after all.
They fought in the war,
To give us more,
Freedom, at our beck and call.

You hear of them being neglected,
In care, and in their own homes.
They may suffer poor sight,
But that doesn't give the right,
To take advantage of their flesh and bones.

There's sexual abuse amongst others,
Where an advance, or touch takes place.
It may go unreported,
And the events get distorted,
When the abused and abuser come face-to-face.

Financial abuse is quite common,
Witholding money to keep them from spending.
But it takes away,
Their ability to pay,
For any extra bits they may have pending.

Psychological abuse is harder to prove,
Comments made can stick in the mind.
When frequently said,
They'll stay in their head,
And they'll dwell on their problems, you'll find.

Physical abuse is easier to spot,
Look for cuts, and bruises, and grazes.
When their clothes are removed,
Observe marks that are not proved,
That they'll try to conceal for ages.

Racial abuse raises its ugly head,
When people's backgrounds don't agree with our own.
They may have different skin,
But they're the same within,
They need support – not left all alone.

If medication is needed,
It should be administered, as the doctor sees fit.
Too much, too late,
Could seal the fate,
Of the person whose life depends on it.

Any suspected abuse should be reported,
Verify facts first, if you possibly can.
Obtain dates and times,
When you spotted the signs,
To protect our elders from their fellow man.

DISTRICT ANGELS

A spasm of pain gripped his body,
As he turned to face the door.
He pulled the blanket tight to his chest,
A bowl close to hand on the floor.

He'd been feeling sick for a couple of days,
Now the pain had got increasingly worse.
He pulled his knees up to the foetal position,
As he waited for the district nurse.

She called to see him, this time each week,
To monitor his independence.
To assess the way he was coping with life,
Knowing too well, he had no dependents.

He grabbed for the bowl, and his body heaved,
But liquid was all he could expel.
He hadn't eaten for a day or two,
Who could he call on? Who could he tell?

The pain was severe in his lower belly,
It hurt him just to breathe.
His head felt hot, and his body shivered,
As, once again, he started to heave.

When the nurse arrived, she let herself in,
He wasn't able to answer the door.
She expected to see him in his chair,
But spotted vomit on the floor.

She could hear his groans from the other room,
Coming from his body on the bed.
She made her way, very warily,
Watching where she could tread.

Her shock was quite apparent,
When she saw his prostrate stance.
She checked his pulse and temperature,
Then phoned for an ambulance.

She knew he shouldn't be at home,
His stomach pains were a worry.
Sickness, she could deal with,
But he needed treatment in a hurry.

It wasn't until late that night,
Doctors voiced what they suspected.
He'd got a stomach ulcer,
That's what the nurse had detected.

He's better off in a hospital ward,
Where he can be watched until he mends.
He can return home once he's better,
To spend time with his friends.

The nurse will resume her visits,
Monitoring closely, every sign.
Thank God she'd called to see him that day,
She'd got to him just in time.

FADED PHOTO'S

I've had the privilege of talking to several men,
During the final months of their life,
And the thing they want to talk about most,
Is the times they spent with their wife.

Usually, they're unable to walk very far,
And are confined to a single armchair.
So they sit, and stare at a photograph,
Of a young woman with flowers in her hair.

The picture is fading, where the sun has shone,
And the frame has seen better days.
It's black and white, but looks sepia at times,
And is the subject of his gaze.

He remembers the time when they married,
They gathered with friends, and family, and more.
To pose for this nostalgic photo,
Before he went off to war.

He tells me that she was a lovely girl,
Who passed away years ago.
She raised a beautiful family,
Amongst the times of woe.

As he sits, just remembering,
About everything that they said,
His mood is rather saddened,
Thinking of the girl he'd wed.

He knows that she's at peace now,
And her pain will hurt no more.
As he prepares, to once again, meet her,
While St. Peter holds open the door!

DYING TO MEET YOU.

I'm not afraid to die,
Let me tell you why,
I'd like to think that I've done right by God.
Though, I don't go to church,
He won't leave me in the lurch,
He won't desert me once he's given me the nod!

I don't believe, God, as a man,
I can't say I'm his biggest fan,
But you must admire his love for all.
I bet he's up there, in the clouds,
Observing his work, and feeling proud,
If he was a party-goer, he'd be having a ball.

He gave Man the ability to choose,
So some will win, and some will lose,
Decisions they make in their daily life.
Some will wander, some will stray,
But mostly, they are likely to stay
With God, whose given support through all their strife.

He takes care of us, when times are rough,
Sometimes he calls another's bluff,
But always he will see us through our ways.
So when my time has come,
I'll be reunited with my mum,
And everyone that went before my days.

It's not the fact of dying,
It's the way you die that's worrying,
Nobody cherishes the thought of pain.
So when I finally depart,
I'll take with me my heart,
And what I leave on Earth, in Heaven, I'll gain.

PILLS… OR PILS!

Let me tell you about a man,
That I visit each weekend.
He suffers from depression,
And on his tablets, does depend.

He lives alone, and stares at the walls,
He can't concentrate on T.V.
His dilemma is growing daily,
And is there for all to see.

Because of the depression,
He likes to have a drink.
Which is followed by another,
Not a good sign, I think.

Now, I know a few of the symptoms,
But I'm not a psychiatrist.
What I do know, is that tablets,
Don't work if you're getting pissed.

His appetite is very poor,
Though a health drink he will take.
It builds up his nutrition,
And will help his food intake.

It's not the drink that makes him depressed,
But depression that makes him drink.
I'd like him to see what it's doing,
And tip his beer down the sink.

Just recently, he has shown some signs,
Of improvement in his ways.
He's started to tidy the living room floor,
That's been rather cluttered for days.

He's taking an interest in programmes,
That are shown on the TV.
Before, he used to watch them,
But he didn't really see.

I'd like to keep this new trend going,
And I've said this to his face.
To make progress with his lifestyle,
And to continue at his pace.

He's got letters that are unanswered,
So I've set him a little task.
To deal with ONE letter by next week,
It's not a lot to ask.

If we can get him to take an interest,
In something other than in his mind,
I'm sure that the results will be significant,
And he can leave his past behind.

THE SAMARITAN

The youth lay in the gutter,
After a fall, on a drinking spree.
He was mumbling something under his breath,
Which sounded like, "Please help me".

He was scruffy, and soaked in urine,
His hair was cut really short,
People went out of their way to avoid him,
Not sparing him a second thought.

Only a few would face the prospect,
Of getting involved in, "Who knows what"!
So they veered away from the drunken lad,
Even though he was in a bit of a spot.

A good Samaritan took his hand,
And helped him to his feet.
He was assisted across the pavement,
And deposited on a seat.

The lad wasn't hurt, but intoxicated,
He'd sober up when the day was done.
How could anyone leave him laying there?
That boy is somebody's son.

His parents need to give him a lecture,
Explaining wrong from right.
Then a repeat, just may not happen,
And he'll never again face this plight.

FORGETFUL

Unable to remember family events,
Where they've been, or what they've done;
Struggling to recall faces,
Can't be a barrel of fun.

Wandering absently, on a whim,
Not knowing their destination;
A growing concern amongst the old,
Spread wide across the nation.

The mind cannot recognise reason,
It seems to operate independently;
The individual seems quite oblivious,
Causing concern for the family.

Dementia comes in many forms,
Slight forgetfulness is the start;
Health regressing with intensity,
Playing a major part.

Constant care and supervision,
A watchful eye on where they go;
Taking note of peculiar outbursts,
As the symptoms steadily grow.

Not responsible for their behaviour,
Living in their own small space;
Confined by the restraints of their mind,
As realism loses pace.

WAIST HIGH

The town was very busy,
Youngsters gathered in the street.
They didn't moderate their language,
It was just a place to meet.

They laughed and shouted, and ran about,
While shoppers felt annoyed.
They pushed and jostled one another,
The girls as bad as boys.

They mocked a girl in a wheelchair,
Her disability, quite apparent.
They verbally threw abuse at her,
Their behaviour, extremely abhorrent.

When challenged by a passing man,
They said, "We don't give a toss.
She's only a bloody cripple;
She's no f**king loss."

The man stood his ground with the troublesome lad,
Til the youth rejoined his mob.
Still shouting obscenities at all around,
Confirming he was just a yob.

The hero turned to the girl in the chair,
And said to the lady, who was pushing her around,
"Is she alright? She's not hurt, I hope–?
She looks like she's found a penny, but lost a pound."

The girl became suddenly offended,
Not by the yobs, but by the mans air.
"I'm a person you know, not a vegetable,
Even though I'm confined to this chair."

When she's being pushed, amid a crowd,
Her face is only waist high.
Yet people talk above her head,
Instead of bending to look in her eyes.

It's bad enough being unable to walk,
Without being treated as a complete misfit.
Being strapped into the invalid chair,
Searching for a comfortable way to sit.

So, if you see someone that's disabled,
Talk to them, at their face height.
Just stoop a little, to bring you down,
To that person's line of sight.

LOST LOVE

She sits by the window on an upright chair,
Staring aimlessly into the sky.
She's all alone in this big, big, world,
And can't for the life of her understand why.

Her eyes are wet, as she inwardly sobs,
Remembering life as it used to be.
She recalls the time with the man she loved,
And the time when their lives were free.

A tear rolls down her pallid cheek,
And moistly stains the blouse she wears.
Her face is sore, where she's dabbed her eyes,
And wiped away the tears.

Her hair is permed, and immaculately styled,
Just the way her husband always admired.
Now she dreams of the bygone days,
And the times that they shared for a while.

But now he's gone, and won't be back,
His illness was too much to bear.
So she sits at the window all day, and recalls,
The years that they once did share.

SLOW, BUT SURE

The hustle and bustle of the crowded street,
Which the elderly traverse with care,
Burdened with their shopping bags,
Bulging with their wares.

They pick their way amongst the throng,
Their stamina put to test.
Heading for the occasional seat,
To give their legs a rest.

Sometimes, armed with a shopping trolley,
They aim for that vacant seat.
But in their quest to reach it,
They knock people's legs and feet.

Lots of ankles take a knock,
But the old 'uns say it's not their fault.
You see, it always pulls over to one side,
It was like it, when it was bought.

They walk at such a sedate pace,
Stopping to chat to folk they meet.
Passing the time of day with anyone,
While blocking up the street.

If you're walking close behind someone,
And they stop to talk to a friend,
You have to swerve to avoid hitting them,
On your instincts, you must depend.

When you find you have to go shopping,
It's best to avoid pension day.
Because once they've got their money,
They'll get in everyone's way.

ACHES AND PAINS

She said, "I must make a confession,
I suffer from depression,
And I don't know how I'm really going to feel.
I get pains inside my head,
As soon as I get out of bed,
And the tension that I suffer, makes me ill.

I get stiffness in my joints,
But to get right to the point,
I think that I am literally falling apart.
My legs are giving me jip,
I've got a sore right hip,
And I've got palpitations with my heart.

My blood pressure is low,
And my urine seems to flow,
Whenever I see water in the sink.
My kidneys sometimes hurt,
When I go to have a squirt,
And my pulse is racing fast, don't you think?

I suffer from diabetes,
And I think the reason for this is,
I eat too many biscuits, sweets and cakes.
I try to cut down on my salt,
But I think it is the fault,
Of the shops that put the stuff into their bakes.

As I totter down the lane,
Leaning heavily on my cane,
I think my aches and pains are here to stay.
I'll keep taking all my pills,
To rid me of my ills,
And I know I'll live to fight another day."

SOLEMN DUTY

The coach glistened, as its highly polished panels reflected the sun,
The windows immaculate, no dirt or water stains that run.

Buffed up at every available chance,
Pristine care and condition, could be seen at a glance.

The shafts were readied for use, and raised,
Two highly groomed mares reversed into place.

Their jet black coats shone proud and bright,
They complemented the coach, in the shimmering light.

Harnesses attached, and the plumes standing high,
On top of their heads, pointing to the sky.

They'd a job to do, so must look their best,
While they carried the coffin, to lay to rest.

Today's task was sensitive, and it was quite clear,
They knew that the cortege would shed a tear.

With a coffin of white, and finished in brass,
The pallbearer had an unenviable task.

With outstretched arms, he supported the casket,
Contrasting against his black, buttoned jacket.

The death of a baby is a solemn affair,
Mourners, and passers-by, stop and stare.

The life had been short to say the least,
So we hope that the child can now Rest In Peace.

THE TIME HAS COME

Nobody came to visit him,
As he lay in his hospital bed.
His condition appeared to be very grim,
As he was constantly being drip-fed.

His bed was opposite the bay I was in,
So I could do nothing but stare.
His chance of survival looked very slim,
As the nurses conducted their care.

He had suffered internal bleeding,
And was in an unconscious state.
The doctors held regular meetings,
Then adjusted his monitoring rate.

I went to sleep, as usual, that night,
But when I awoke the next day,
I guess the poor man had lost his fight,
For they'd taken his bed away.

The bay was bare of his personal things,
His belongings had all been taken.
A new bed was made in this medical wing,
That was available for the next patient.

The way the nurses deal with times like this,
Must depress them, and make them feel low.
To clear up after a loss, isn't everyone's wish,
But they are prepared, when it's time to go.

RESPECT

I'd like to bring to people's attention,
The good work that carers perform.
They are put into a situation,
Doing jobs that are not the norm.

They fight against the traffic,
To reach their calls when needed.
They seldom receive any thanks,
Though they've battled, and succeeded.

Usually, they know what they'll face,
And are prepared for the task.
But sometimes the unexpected is encountered,
They'll do it without being asked.

Not everybody will change people's dirty pads,
Or put them onto a commode.
Clean them up, when they've finished,
And leave them comfortable in their homes.

Who would choose to clean up sick?
That's been spilled on the floor.
By somebody unable to tend to themselves,
An unexpected chore.

A wheelchair bound man or woman,
Who can't fend for themselves at all.
Will eagerly wait for their carer,
To tend to their needs when they call.

Just a little chat is a comfort,
For many a lonely person.
But they're monitoring the situation,
Of their safety, they're making certain.

Occasionally, you get the odd people,
That don't accept the things that are done.
They feel that the carers should be like robots,
Always serious, with no sense of fun.

But it's hard to face a person who's ill,
Who puts up with pain seven days a week.
It's with them all of their waking hours,
And all of the time they're asleep.

A little light-hearted banter is welcome,
As it brings a relief to their life.
Not for long, I must admit,
But it eases some of their strife.

So please accept the carers,
Who travel in all kinds of weather,
To get to the ill and unfortunate,
Who just want to look after others.

They do their best to help folk,
Working within an established plan.
But that unexpected event can happen,
To any woman or man!

FINAL MOMENTS

His pallid features were a contrast,
To the duvet on the bed.
The floral pattern, brightly coloured,
On the pillow, beneath his head.

His eyes were closed as he peacefully slept,
Often, for a very short respite.
Then the pain would return to break his calm,
And he'd grimace in the room's dimmed light.

His appetite for food had long since gone,
And he would never, ever, complain.
But occasionally a spasm would tear him apart,
As his body was racked with pain.

His wife sat quietly by his side,
His family waited downstairs.
It's time like this that folk rally round,
And show just how much they care.

She stroked his hand, and mopped his brow,
More for her sake, than his.
When he's lying there, what can you do?
She stooped to give him a kiss.

His breathing was shallow, and fading away,
As she looked at the love of her life.
He seemed peaceful, as she glanced at the card on the shelf,
"GET WELL SOON"…from your loving wife.

She knew the day would come quite soon,
When his last breath would take him away.
The inevitable passing of one that's loved,
Oh, how she wished he could stay.

They'd been together through thick and thin,
Through good times, and the bad.
To see him lying there, close to death,
Made her feel extremely sad.

She couldn't stand the thought of him suffering more,
And his passing would make the pain go.
She wiped a lone tear that had formed in her eye,
Her distress must never show.

A gasp... then a twitch from his horizontal form,
His head slightly rolled to one side.
His eyes were closed, as though in sleep,
But from this world, he did gently glide.

The family attended their father's bedside,
When she called them up the stairs.
They expressed their love, and regrets, with tears,
And the sorrow that they all shared.

CARERS

Learning to care for others,
    In the comfort of their own home;
Once age or ill health overtakes them,
    And they are left all alone.

Never demanding much from others,
    Now their working life is done;
Determined to keep fighting,
    Til their race is finally run.

Only grit and determination,
    Will help to see them through,
Now carers can give assistance,
    In the form of me and you.

Care and consideration do not cost much,
    A little help with personal tasks;
A kind word, an ear, and a cup of tea,
    Are not too much to ask.

Repaying a debt to society,
    For their efforts in conflicts past,
Every person working for London Care,
    Dedicated, to the last!

GOODBYE MY LOVE

In the afternoon shade, offered by the dusty, ragstone wall,
I kneel by the marble plaque; remembering you before you answered
Our Maker's call.

The stained glass of the windows, reaching high into the sky,
If I stare intensely, I can just make out some figures, if I really try.

But from within the church those windows come alive;
With the sun shining through, there's proof that we will survive.

Life remains sacred, preserved for eternity in some other form;
Not always recognisable, as that person we loved, since the day that
We were born.

Stories unfold from the coloured mosaic within its leaded frames,
Jesus, the son of God, with those well known Biblical names.

He was the Michael Parkinson, a meeter and greeter of his day,
Talking to people, and teaching them how to lead their lives God's
Way.

Vases of flowers, great bouquets arranged magnificently, ornate the
Aisles;
While the altar reflects the light from that symbolic cross, and all that
It implies.

Your resting place, between this world and beyond is in a prime
Location;
A spot of beauty, made even more perfect by your situation.

The cultivated flower beds, tended so well by the ecclesiastical staff,
And the neatly trimmed grass between headstones that skirt the path.

Years of movement beneath the soil, and winds that blow so strong
Make tombs subside, and nestle at irregular angles, for people now
Long gone.

A final resting place? I'm not so sure, but a place for me to sit;
I think of this more as a place you've stopped, so I can come to visit.

You'll continue your journey without me, though I'll catch you up
Some day,
But for now I'll talk in the shade of the wall, where unfortunately,
You couldn't stay.

I feel your presence, every time I enter this place,
Knowing that you're with me, though I can't see your face.

In my mind, you'll never age, you'll stay young forever as I remember
You;
But I'll visit, and talk, and tell you the news of the folk that you once
Knew.

One day soon, when my time on Earth has reached its destination,
We'll meet up, wherever you are, and continue our conversation.

I've got lots I want to tell you; much I should have said when you
Were here,
But it'll keep, I'm sure the stories you can tell will be greater to the
Ear.

So goodbye my love, til next we meet, on some future day;
I know you must be busy, I'll let you get on your way.

I don't know what's facing you daily, in the existence you've now
Applied,
But feel free of any burdens that you had, when you were alive.

Section 13

SOME YOU WIN

ANUS HORRIBILIS

When you go out shopping,
And you want to use the loo;
You'll find the shop you're in ain't got one,
So you won't know what to do.

You can ask if you can use their one,
But they'll say it's just for staff;
When you explain it's very urgent,
They'll shake their heads and laugh.

So, off you trot, out of the door,
You find you have to leave the shop.
Wandering through the precinct,
Not daring to stop.

Walking with your knees together,
Keeping your buttocks clenched tight;
Makes you quite conspicuous,
Everyone can guess your plight.

As you enter the public toilets,
You join the end of the queue;
Full of people with their legs crossed,
Waiting to use the loo.

You shuffle along quite slowly,
Til you are next in line;
You dive into the cubicle,
Only just in time.

A sigh of relief is heard from afar,
At the end of this comical caper;
But you'll find that your troubles are not over,
There's probably no paper!

JASON

I used to take the dog for a walk,
Let him off the lead for a run.
He'd scamper about,
And without a doubt,
You could tell he was having fun.

Actually, he was my brother's dog,
But as time went by, we found
We all loved him more,
That golden labrador,
That intelligent, obedient hound.

We'd go for miles in the countryside,
Up hills, amongst the trees.
He'd chase rabbits galore,
Across the woodland floor,
In fact, anything he sees.

He'd return to the house, panting, and gasping for breath,
But his approach just didn't alter.
After coming home,
He'd expect a bone,
And a dish of cooling water.

He'd slurp and lap it, making a mess,
His aim was pure "hit and miss".
Food and water spread around,
And then we found,
He'd want to give us a kiss.

If you've never kissed a slobbering dog,
Nor when he's finished drinking, either,
You won't know what I mean,
When I say, "he's keen",
To get you dripping with his saliva.

It's only a show of affection,
His way of showing gratitude.
If you dare push him away,
Then another day,
He'll bring you his bone... half chewed.

We loved that dog called Jason,
He became a family friend.
When we took him out,
Without a doubt,
On him, we knew we could depend.

Always faithful to his keepers,
Returning friendship every day,
But as time passed,
He reached his last,
As his life gradually ebbed away.

Numerous visits to the vet's surgery,
Confirmed that he'd just got old.
We'd had him for ages,
But through all of those stages,
We'd kept photos, as his life did unfold.

My memories linger, deep down inside,
But once I start to recall;
The times we had,
I'm so very glad,
That he'd enjoyed his time with us all.

DONATIONS GRATEFULLY ACCEPTED

We'd like you to donate money,
Any amount you can give;
To assist those poorer than yourself,
Basically, to help them live.

If you can only spare a few pennies,
We'll give our thanks to you;
The value of all those little coins,
Will gradually accrue.

Forget the administration,
We'll not pass on the costs,
There's too much poverty in this world,
Too many lives are lost.

Too many charities to choose from?
Pick a cause close to your heart;
Look at the work that it achieves,
That's a good place to start.

You can drop your money into a box,
Or pay it in at the banks;
It'll all go to a worthy cause,
For your donation, we give you our thanks.

RECYCLING

Green glass, brown glass,
And clear glass bins;
A place to dispose of
Any old tins.

Clothes and shoes
No longer a fit;
Recycle – don't send
To a landfill pit.

Newspapers gathered
By the score;
On a daily basis,
Accumulate more.

Cardboard boxes
Folded flat;
Easier handled
When not so fat.

Plastic bottles
From many a source;
Separated from rubbish,
As a matter of course.

It's our duty to dispose
Of the stuff we accrue;
So take time to sort it,
I'm begging you.

Maybe, this Planet
In the years ahead,
Will be thanking you
For not leaving it… dead!

SOME YOU WIN!

"Congratulations… you're a winner,"
Said the voice on the telephone.
I wish that they'd stop ringing me,
I want to be left alone.

How can I be a winner,
When I've entered no competition?
But still they keep on calling,
With monotonous repetition.

I'm afraid I lose my temper,
I can be abrupt, and verbally rude,
If they disturb my relaxation time,
With their insistence to intrude.

I know they're only doing their job,
Promoting services, to numbers they're fed;
But why can't they just leave me alone,
And ring somebody else instead?

EASY PARKING

The busy car park has marked out bays,
So vehicles can be left by the score.
Spaced regularly, so people can get out of their cars,
Without fear of knocking their doors.

Some bays are wide for disabled drivers,
Others are for families unloading pushchairs.
But drivers find these are easier to use,
When parking their 4 X 4's.

They swerve across lines, marking out the bays,
And leave their vehicles all askew.
Not satisfied with driving like lunatics,
They'll take up the space for two.

Obviously not disabled, nor with a child,
They're oblivious to where they park.
They cross the street to go to the shops,
Or into the pub, until after dark.

It's usually a burly builder type bloke,
With a beer belly hanging over his belt.
Wearing a tight fitting T-shirt,
Perspiring, like he's starting to melt.

He wouldn't have a clue as to the distress caused,
Or inconvenience he'd managed to create.
As long as he can park his gigantic car,
He'll resign you to your fate.

Trying to talk to him would be pointless,
It really would be no use,
Because all you'd get as his reply,
Is a lot of verbal abuse.

CREATIVE CANVAS

If I was to paint a picture,
No matter how hard I tried,
There's no way I could ever match,
The beauty of the morning sky.

A watercolour wash to lay the base,
Then build up tones, in-between;
Layer upon layer of tinted hues,
To imitate the scene.

Swathes of yellow, a stroke of the brush,
As the sun begins to rise;
Pinks and greys are prominent,
In the early skies.

The air is still, very little breeze,
In the distance, a hot air balloon glides high;
A contrast to the canvas that
I've painted in my mind's eye.

Skimming silhouetted tree tops,
Canada geese on their morning vacation,
Regular as clockwork, every day,
In a predictable "V" formation.

Not even the most talented artist,
With his skills, could manage to capture,
The true beauty of that morning sky,
As produced by Mother Nature.

QUAYSIDE

As I strolled on the quayside, the wind blew strong,
It was daybreak, and the gulls barked their call.
Swooping to the surface of the water,
As it buffeted against the wall.

The clanging of the boats, as they bobbed about,
And the slap of their ropes against hulls.
Multi-coloured oil slicks swirled about,
And were parted by the dive of the gulls.

A seafront café was preparing for trade,
Bacon smells wafted through the air.
Anglers, burdened with rods and holdalls,
Had a regular meeting place there.

A hot cup of tea, and a fry-up meal,
To set their day on the right track.
Then board the boats, and head out to sea,
Planning what to do with their catch.

Brave pedestrians appeared with collars turned high,
To protect from the bracing air.
Dogs scampered ahead, sniffing all in sight,
As shops prepared to display their ware.

Buckets and spades, lilos, and colourful hats,
Were hung from all available hooks.
Postcards and toys, and sticks of rock,
With ice cream, candy floss, and books.

Holidaymakers were needed to spend their cash,
Now that the day had begun.
The season too short for the stallholders,
Who had to rely on the sun.

NOCTURNAL NOISES

The shrill screeching in the darkened fields,
Echo in the dead of night.
Wildlife on their nocturnal prowl,
Glimpsed briefly in the moonlight.

Foxes, sounding like a child in pain,
High-pitched howling, like somebody hurt.
Calling out to other foxes
From their holes, burrowed in the earth.

Owls, calling from the tree tops,
Rhythmic, like a metronome.
Evenly spaced, in deep, husky hootings,
In their guttural, dulcet tones.

Occasionally, an unusual sound,
A beast lets out a noise.
Different in pitch from all of the others,
A barking in its voice.

At the earliest signs of daylight,
The noises will have ceased.
So the secrets of the dark hours,
Will remain safely with the beasts.

BOOT FAIRS

Cars and vans lined up in a row,
Across the field, some with trailers in tow.

They set up their wares on a pasting table,
Displaying goods, the best they are able.

Clothes go onto a hanging rail,
With tickets to show the price of the sale.

The table withstands the china and glass,
While kiddies toys are strewn over the grass.

Tools have been taken from garden sheds,
Trays of flowers waiting to be planted in beds.

Records and CD's, and videos galore,
Scrutinized by collectors, clamouring for more.

Electrical goods, some rather old,
Reduced in price to ensure they're sold.

Furniture items in need of repair,
Wigs made out of unnatural hair.

Ice cream and burger vans do a roaring trade,
Counting the cash from the sales they've made.

A delight for the family on a Sunday morning,
To rummage the goods sheltered beneath the awnings.

If you can't find something that you seek,
Don't worry… there'll be new stalls here next week!

PIGEON FANCIER

Sometimes, when you wake up,
And you have your breakfast food,
It doesn't take long to realise,
You're in a very good mood.

Your spirits are instantly lifted,
Like a pigeon flying high;
Looking down on all beneath you,
With the freedom of the sky.

Other days, you don't feel like moving,
When you wake, you feel like grot!
You want to spend time in solitude,
Like a statue, glued to the spot.

We all have to face one thing in life,
And that, you can't deny;
Some days, when you're like a statue,
Look out for pigeons, dropping packages from the sky.

The moral of this story is,
When you're on top, it's a feeling of might!
When you're down, someone is above you,
Sh**ing on you, from a very great height!

A HOME OF IT'S OWN

Every morning, around seven o'clock,
Just as it was getting light;
I observed a visit from a blackbird,
On a regular course of flight.

It flew onto my garage roof,
Then swooped to the rotary line;
Hopped onto the garden fence,
The same route, every time.

It hesitated for a while,
Then guardedly looked around,
When satisfied that the coast was clear,
Entered a bush that it had found.

I didn't want to frighten it,
But thought it must have a nest in there;
I took a look one evening,
And saw a matting of fine hair.

The bird had laid foundations,
Woven fibres, with beak and claw;
A base on which to build its nest,
Twigs held it steady, and secure.

In all, it only took three weeks,
The sides formed a bowl, as the nest was grown;
Ingenuity and dexterity of the blackbird,
Had built a home to call its own.

THE MILKMAN

The milkman starts work early,
Manoeuvring his vehicle through the estates.
Travelling at a snail's pace,
Carrying lots of rattling crates.

He'll put the brakes on anywhere,
In the centre of the road.
Blocking all the traffic,
Ignoring the Highway Code.

He hops out of his moving cab,
And runs round to the back.
I'm sure, if known, he'd get told off,
Possibly even get the sack.

Bottles of milk in each of his hands,
A loaf of bread tucked under his arm.
A box of eggs, and orange juice,
The milk fresh from the farm.

He runs along the garden paths,
And right up to the door.
Back again to move the float,
Then do the same once more.

Where would we be without him,
And the services he provides?
Getting daily milk to pensioners,
Who, in their homes must bide.

Somehow, he manages to get through,
No matter what the weather brings.
You'll find your milk on the doorstep,
Along with all the other things.

ROOT CANAL

Today on the TV news,
They showed ducks that were confused,
Mistaking a local canal for a farmer's field.
From a distance it could be seen,
Looking like a bowling green,
But the water down below was being concealed.

The reason they couldn't tell,
Was due to the hot spell,
The duckweed on the surface grew quite dense.
It caused intense stagnation,
And starved the water of oxygenation,
As the depth of the weed proved immense.

It clogged up propellers on the boats,
And anything that usually floats,
It hinders little ducklings learning to swim.
By sticking to their feet,
They can't paddle quick enough to beat,
The suction of the roots that grow within.

They say the canal will soon be cleared,
Once the hot spell's disappeared,
And the duckweed won't survive the colder weathers.
But for now, ducks must decide,
Although the waterway is wide,
Do they really want this sticking to their feathers.

TSUNAMI

Devastation hit the country,
When a wave submerged the town;
Obliterating all the buildings,
That were spread for miles around.

Movement from plates beneath the sea
Caused a tidal wave;
Which grew with such intensity,
That nothing in its path could be saved.

People watched in horror
As the giant wave approached;
A wall rising from the ocean,
Changing the horizon as it encroached.

Chaos and mayhem ensued ashore,
As they clamoured to reach higher ground;
But apart from high rise hotels,
There was nowhere to be found.

A tremendous roar like thunder,
As the wave crashed on the land;
Taking with it boats and dwellings,
Spread along the sand.

Trees were felled, buildings washed away,
Mud engulfed all in sight;
Boats travelled hundreds of yards inland,
Survivors petrified with fright.

Then nothing… a quietness… no roaring wave,
The sound of screaming split the air;
Families had been ripped apart,
Washed away to God knows where!

The stillness didn't last for long,
As the water that had snapped down trees,
While drowning all on its way inland,
Returned to the depth of the seas.

Debris picked up from land based areas
Hit the town, from the other side;
Trees, furniture, huts and rubble,
Were carried on the returning tide.

Thousands of people not yet accounted for,
Children ripped from their bed;
Elderly, unable to get out of the way,
Able bodied, all now feared dead.

Only foundations remained of local''s homes,
Roads vanished from the scene;
The changing face of their little town,
Left rubble where their homes had been.

Boats, once used for fishing,
Now inland, wedged in branches of trees;
While crops from inland plantations,
Now were food for the seas.

The loss of life reached colossal figures,
As aid poured in from far and wide;
Help to restore the primitive town,
Devastated by that tide.

TOURIST DISTRACTION

They gather in the High Street
Where the road adjoins The Brook;
They seem to be there any time of day.
About four or five unsavouries,
Mixed sexes, race and creeds,
Obstructing shoppers, and getting in the way.

Monopolising the wooden benches,
Where shoppers could have a rest,
And take the weight off of their tired feet;
These people sprawl, and sit, and argue
In slurred but roaring voices,
Staking their claim to that High Street seat.

Bottles gathered by their feet,
Kicked, and rolling on the path,
Amongst a vast assortment of beer cans;
They stagger to and fro,
Opinions shouted, loud and crude,
The drink never leaves their clutching hands.

It doesn't make an appealing sight,
To people passing by,
Or traders who are trying to sell their wares;
But nothing seems to be getting done,
To stop this meeting taking place,
In fact, nobody from the council really cares.

Where is authority when it's needed?
It's certainly not in Chatham,
As they seem to congregate most every day;
If these drunks are not moved on,
Regeneration can't take place,
This tourist attraction won't encourage visitors to stay.

RESILIENCE

When the whole world seems on your shoulders,
And nobody seems to care,
Your mouth is dry, and you want to cry,
You feel in the depth of despair.

When the people you thought were friendly,
Metaphorically stick knives in your back,
You have no choice, but to bear their voice,
Shrug your shoulders and take the flak.

When you feel a lump in your throat,
And you resent having to show respect;
Let them play their games, call you names,
Treat them all with circumspect.

They'll tire of being so childish,
If your resilience they can't break down;
So until that day, let them have their way,
Just stare at them blankly, and frown.

You need to retain your composure,
Count to ten, and keep walking tall;
But under your breath, you can curse them to death,
And inwardly say, "F**k them all!"

THINGS ARE LOOKING UP

If you stare at the sky for long enough,
Your head will start to spin,
Until you gradually lose your balance,
And feel quite sick within.

The clouds are always moving,
Like a kaleidoscope in the sky.
Forming pictures, ever changing,
You can see them if you try.

When looking up, you see no land,
No horizons on which to focus.
Only the sky to fill your view,
And the occasional cumulus-nimbus.

You can feel your body swaying,
And want to hold on tight,
To something that is firmly fixed;
To shield your eyes from the light.

When you turn away, you'll see sunspots,
Even when your eyes are closed.
Flashing and spinning inside your head,
As your vision becomes composed.

Those pictures hiding amongst the clouds,
Can be seen when the weather's fair.
For imagination is a wonderful thing,
You can see things that are not there!

FREEBIES

I've been given several CDs
That came free with the papers.
Some films are really serious,
Others are comedy capers.

The films are generally past their best,
Though were quite good in their day,
But as I've already seen them,
I think I'll give them away.

Somebody will enjoy them,
If they haven't seen them before.
I'll put the others to one side,
If I get any more.

They're all too good to throw away,
For some folk, they'd be fun.
They came with The Express and Daily Mail,
The Mirror, and The Sun.

It's just a little gift they add,
From the paper to you and me,
But the biggest bonus of them all,
Is that they are absolutely free!

ROADSIDE FAIRIES

Nestled amongst the grass on the roadside banks,
A delicate white head can be found;
On a moist filled stem, of whitish green,
Standing a few inches from the ground.

A favourite for children to casually pick,
And hold up to face height;
Its head an aura, so fragile,
Of interlocking stems – a magnificent sight.

A great deep breath, then blow out their cheeks,
Watch the flimsy spores rise in the air;
Floating, in suspended motion,
Drifting without a care.

Dandelions, now transformed from their yellow blooms,
Are equally as beautiful, in their new found form;
Riding on Mother Nature's breath,
Like a fairy, newly born.

Section 14

STOP... AND THINK

OUT WITH A BANG!

If you want to get work experience,
And are a total newcomer,
The one job you needn't apply for,
Is that of a suicide bomber.

If your tutor is good at his teaching,
He'd have experience of his own;
But then he wouldn't be able to instruct you,
More than his cover, would be blown.

No, a suicide bomber must be self taught,
Or learn from someone who's failed;
Whose ideas of retribution,
Have come off the rails.

With minds twisted like the wreckage,
More than sanity can take,
Amongst debris and mutilation,
Left in a successful mission's wake.

A suicide bomber has no future prospects,
Chances of promotion are thin on the ground.
But they'll try to piece together your epitaph,
If your exploded body parts, can all be found.

WHY?

Why does the sun keep shining?
To brighten the lives of us all,
When its rays burn our skin,
And fibres within,
From the heat of that great fiery ball.

Why does the sun keep shining?
When the hot countries all seem at war,
They kill and they maim,
But what is their aim?
What the hell are these conflicts for?

Why does the sun keep shining?
It brings chaos to our motorways.
The surge to the beach,
And the aim to reach,
A tan on the hottest of days.

If the sun could rest from shining,
For its heat can be so intense,
Perhaps everyone,
Could enjoy the fun,
And warring nations regain some sense.

A TEASE

That little dress, I must confess,
Excites me every day;
So don't pretend, you don't comprehend,
When I say it gets me this way.

When I see you walk, it's hard to talk,
My mouth goes completely dry;
When I hear your voice, I have no choice,
My feelings, I must deny.

When you touch my hand, I don't understand,
Quite what you're trying to say;
If I stroke your hair, I get nowhere,
And you gently move away.

I use all of my charm, to take your arm,
But my advances you choose to spurn;
I encircle your waist, but it's not to your taste,
As you remove my hand, and then turn.

I give you a smile, and all the while,
I'm trying out all of the moves;
I give your bottom a squeeze, I think you're a tease,
Perhaps I'd better ply you with booze.

You're lovely to look at, you're not too fat,
Your breasts are a perfect pair;
I'd better leave you alone, I won't even phone,
It seems I can only stare!

ARE WE THERE YET?

When you set off on your holidays,
The luggage in the boot of the car;
The journey ahead is daunting,
You've never before driven that far.

You recently passed your driving test,
So, strapped the kids into their seats,
Made notes of the roads you need to take,
As a celebratory treat.

Your partner is a good companion,
Who never gets in a flap.
Someone to give you directions,
While studying the map.

It won't be long before you hear
Murmuring from the kids, I bet;
When they ask that monotonous question,
"Are we nearly there yet?"

The first time, it's quite funny,
As you get into your stride;
Concentrating on the traffic,
Your frustration, you try to hide.

You stick to the limits of the road,
While other vehicles hurtle past.
Breaking rules and regulations,
Any false move could be your last!

A white knuckle ride as you grip the wheel,
Concentration etched on your face.
Staring at the road ahead,
As past you, others race.

The kids are getting edgy,
Their boredom starting to show;
Still wanting a sensible answer,
"How much further to go?"

It's been a tiring journey,
The kids have driven you insane;
You've only got a few days rest,
Then you can do it all over again.

POLITICAL CORRECTNESS

Golliwogs, were the black-faced dolls,
That children used to love, and adore.
But now we have to call them Gollies,
We can't say the full name anymore.

The rhyme of Baa Baa Black Sheep,
Was renamed, in case it offended.
Baa Baa Rainbow Sheep, doesn't sound right,
But we're told that's how it's amended.

What if you've got a spot on your face?
Can we still call it a blackhead?
Or do we have to refer to it,
As something else instead?

What about a blackbird?
It's called that, because of its shade.
We are not trying to offend it,
When a reference to colour is made.

Why is a newspaper printed with black ink?
Should they try dark paper, and print in white?
At least it would help with one thing,
You'd be able to read it at night!

It's out of hand, this Political Correctness,
As we try not to embarrass coloured folk.
I'm sure they are not really offended,
And find the whole thing a bit of a joke.

CHAT ROOMS

You log onto a chat room,
Scan the names upon the screen;
Join in a conversation,
With someone you've never seen.

They say that they are still at school,
And talk of childish things;
Ask who your favourite band is;
What's the name of the boy that sings?

Enthuse about your Christmas gifts,
Your friends, and what you do;
Where you go at weekends,
And who goes along with you.

They ask the colour of your eyes,
And how long is your hair?
Is it straight or curly?
Is it dark or fair?

You give this information,
And receive some in reply;
Gradually building a mental image,
Of your friend, in your mind's eye.

BEWARE... somewhere in a lonely room,
Could sit a dangerous man;
Talking to young children,
The way young children can.

Is this the man YOU'RE talking to?
Not the person that you thought;
But a pervert preying on the under-aged,
Who really needs to be caught.

If you ever get suspicious,
Then tell your mum and dad;
Of anything you're not sure of,
He could be really bad.

There are some naughty men out there,
Who will gain your confidence,
By talking to you sweetly,
Sometimes leaving you in suspense.

Don't be fooled by their attitude,
Don't believe in all they tell;
For beneath their constant stream of lies,
All is far from well.

IF ONLY!

I'd like a bit of toast for breakfast,
At the very start of day.
I'd smother it with butter,
And then in marmalade.

I'd wash it down with hot, sweet tea.
As soon as the day breaks.
Then a bowl of something sugary,
Like Crunchy Nut Cornflakes.

I'd take my lunchbox, packed for work,
Full of crisps and choc bars,
Bounty, Aero and Milky Way,
Plus Fudge, Snickers and Mars.

When I get home after a day of toil,
I'd have fish and chips for dinner.
With lashings of salt to give it taste,
Does that really make me a sinner?

For the evening I'd have a few sandwiches,
To ease my tastebuds fears.
Then sluice it down with a couple of cans,
Of lovely, ice-cool beers.

I bet you think my eating style,
If I ate like this, is pathetic.
But really, I eat like a good boy,
Because, unfortunately, I'm diabetic!

TWO MINUTES OF YOUR TIME

A simple effigy of a red poppy,
To symbolise what has gone before,
Commemorating British servicemen
Who gave their lives in the War.

Hand to hand combat, in the trenches,
The killing fields, knee deep in mud and slime;
Thousands died miles away from home,
In those distant, harrowing times.

The intervention of tanks and aircraft,
Killed more with their direct hits;
As the powerful weapons obliterated,
Cities and towns in later conflicts.

Ships went down to the bottom of the sea,
Never to be seen again;
Taking with them, the bodies of hundreds
Of fighting, family men.

Battles are still ongoing,
Each day, killing more and more;
Our troops are facing danger,
In the current desert war.

So, just spare two minutes of your time,
Stop what you're doing, and pray to heaven;
Wear a poppy to remember the heroes, lost,
At 11 am, on Eleven – Eleven.

THAT'S A COMPLIMENT?

"Shall I compare thee to a Summer's Day?"
Not in this country, mate;
If I tried to make a comparison,
It would surely seal your fate.

A Summers day in England
Is a relatively safe bet;
That sometime in those twenty-four hours,
You're going to get very wet.

The sunshine never lasts for long,
It vanishes all too soon;
Leaving behind it, in its wake
A day of doom and gloom.

When it is dry for a day or two,
And you feel like going for a jog;
Take a compass to get your bearings,
Before you get lost in the smog.

Exhaust fumes and untreated pollution,
Fill the Summer air with a haze;
How quickly it obscures the vision,
Its intensity can only amaze.

So, the twit that compares you to a Summer day,
Should think twice, before making this quip;
Insinuating that you're dull and dismal,
In fact, he means you're a bit of a drip!

WAR ZONE

The melancholy dirge rang out,
Across the city square;
Bodies retrieved from desecrated homes,
Amongst choking dust clouds, in the air.

The wailing of the women,
As their missing men were found;
Mutilated, and bloodied torsos
Unearthed from the rubbled ground.

Family men, only this morning,
Going to work, like any day;
Never returning to see their loved ones,
With their children, they'll never play.

Yet, they chose to take up weapons,
To protect what little they had;
What use were hand guns, and rifles?
The idea that they could win was mad.

If the missiles that pounded their city,
Had been aimed the other way;
The fighting men from the community,
Would live another day.

But no direct hits every time,
Causing mayhem, and devastation;
And all because of excessive greed,
By the larger, invading nation.

Carcasses pieced together by aid workers,
Where they were blown, limb from limb;
Wooden boxes, and bags at the ready,
To put the body parts in.

Trenches, cut into the dusty earth,
Boxes laid in a line;
A great loss to this small community,
Praying for a peaceful time.

But no matter how much they want it,
And no matter how they try;
Peace seems to bypass these people,
The children look on, and cry.

Will they ever see peace in their lifetime?
And know freedom, to come and go?
Until both sides get together, and talk,
I guess we will never know!

"LOOK JOHN, LOOK"

We teach our children at an early age,
To read from a "Janet and John" book.
They start with the names of the characters,
Then go on to "Look John, Look".

Whoever decided to use the name John?
They should have used Fred, or Sam or equivalent.
It's confusing enough, when teaching adults,
Because the "H" in John, is silent.

Even if a child is taught phonetically,
The "H" still wouldn't be used.
So why is it there in the first place?
It'll leave the child totally confused.

YOU'RE WORRIED?

Whenever you've got worries,
And you feel you want to frown;
The world seems on your shoulders,
The smallest things get you down.

When there doesn't seem to be an end,
To the problems that you've got,
Just take some time to sit a while,
And contemplate your lot.

Some people live in terror,
Of weather, explosions and war,
Never knowing what will face them,
If they step outside their door.

Floods demolish houses,
And earthquakes crack the lands;
While people fleeing to save their lives,
Shelter in anything that stands.

Missiles firing overhead,
As warring nations fight to the death;
Destroying the military and civilians,
All in the same breath.

So when you think your problems,
Are too much to surmount;
And all those little niggling things,
Are too numerous to count;

Stop a while to think of those,
Whose world could end today;
Stripped of all their innocence,
Their lives just thrown away.

What have they done to deserve it?
Their existence isn't so bad;
Trying to preserve their dignity,
And the few possessions they had.

Retaliation by the armed forces,
When somebody makes the strike first;
Only escalates when they are targeted,
And the situation only gets worse.

It's difficult to get a ceasefire,
When everything is out of hand.
Each side blaming one another,
For destroying their homeland.

But think about the people,
Women and children, and the old;
Sheltering in the ruins,
Not moving until they're told.

Their homes annihilated,
No water or sanitation;
Food and medicines running out,
In total devastation.

So just a moment of your time,
To contemplate, and sit;
Think of other's problems,
Your's isn't so bad... is it?

SOD IT!

I thought I'd buggered up my printer,
I know it's all my fault;
I put a brand new cartridge,
Somewhere I didn't ought!

I was in a bit of a hurry,
Took the cartridge from the pack;
Removed the old one from the printer,
And pushed the new one back.

I didn't feel any resistance,
But a message on the screen,
Said the wrong cartridge had just been installed,
Something I hadn't foreseen.

In my haste, I'd unwrapped a black one,
Pushed it into the colour port;
I really should've kept it separate,
From the others that I'd bought.

I pulled and tugged at the bloody thing,
But still it would not release;
I failed to get it from the hole,
It proved to be a beast.

Ink now covered my fingers,
As I tried to get a grip;
No matter how I tried it,
It somehow managed to slip.

Then, as I was about to give it up,
And ease all of my frustration,
It suddenly came out in my hand,
Much to my satisfaction.

I replaced it with the right one,
Made sure it went in the right slot;
Didn't want to get it mixed up,
With the others that I've got.

When I tried the printer,
Much to my relief,
It whirled into action straight away,
And gave me no more grief.

I think I've learned my lesson,
Next time I won't push my luck;
If I take my time installing it,
Hopefully, it won't get bloody stuck!

KINKS, LYNX, AND STUFF THAT STINKS

I'll tell you a little story,
Exaggerated, but basically true;
About some funny goings on,
Down at Howlett's Zoo.

A man I know talks in his sleep,
He mumbled something the other night;
It wasn't easy to understand,
And was overheard by his wife.

He said he fancied a little pussy,
And being locked in a cage;
His wife thought he was a pervert,
And flew into a rage.

The image boiled up inside her,
He was never a tiger in bed,
But she couldn't rid it from her mind,
All day it filled her head.

That night, she confronted her husband,
About his little kinks;
Said he should be thrown to the lions,
Pumas, tigers, cougar and lynx.

When she finished hitting him,
He said his actions were pure;
He'd been dreaming of the feline cats,
Of that, she could be sure.

His wish had always been to work,
With big cats at a zoo;
To spend time cleaning, and tending them,
In everything they do.

His wife was apologetic,
She'd had a terrible fright;
When she heard him talking,
In the middle of the night.

She made a couple of phone calls,
Using the mobile he'd bought her;
Trying to contact friends and relatives,
Finally telephoning his daughter.

They rang the office at Howlett's Zoo,
To see if there was a way,
He could spend some time, as a special treat,
And be a keeper for the day.

They happily agreed to arrange it,
And said, that in their eyes,
To film and record this one-off day,
Would be very wise.

So that's what's going to happen,
He'll need a nerve of iron,
To go in with the big cats,
And come face to face with a lion.

But just in case he had been lying,
And said this on a whim,
There was always a chance the big cats,
Would tear him limb from limb!!!!!

PLANE TO SEE

I watch the aeroplanes sail through the clouds,
Vapour trails criss-crossing the azure gaps.
A small speck, ahead of that chalk-like line,
Heading for countries, scattered wide on the maps.

Business men, controlling their empires,
Working, while up in the sky.
In touch with their destinations,
Looking down on the world from on high.

Families, with excited children,
On their way to some far off land.
Facing two weeks of continuous sunshine,
The dream holiday, for which they'd planned.

When I look, I can't help but wonder,
Just where the aircraft will touch down.
Discharging its cargo of tourists,
In some distant, foreign town.

I find it very hard to imagine,
That tiny speck is only one jet.
But the sky is filled with thousands,
Each filled with bodies, I bet!

So, with all those people above me,
Over my head, like birds on the wing;
Each enjoying their flight to somewhere,
Makes me think of only one thing.

I know, exactly, what my weight is,
For the thousands flying, let's multiply,
Then add the mass of the aircrafts;
How the hell do they stay in the sky???

NO TUNNEL VISION

The rhythm of the speeding train,
As it hurtles along the track,
Aware of the time of your meeting,
Don't want to get the sack.

Sit with your back towards the engine,
So you can see where you've been;
Trees and houses rushing past,
Disappearing from the scene.

Try to read your magazine,
Finding it hard to concentrate;
Should have left home earlier,
Must be in the office by eight.

Check the papers in your briefcase,
All seem to be in order;
No major hold-ups so far,
As the train crosses the county border.

It's stuffy in the carriage,
You need to clear your head;
Lean out of the lowered window,
In an instant, you are DEAD!!!

Decapitated by the brickwork,
Forming the tunnel wall;
Your head severed from your shoulders,
Like a bouncing ball.

Your torso slumps back in the carriage,
Blood gushing everywhere;
Covering door and windows,
And seats that others share.

No need to worry about your appointment,
The train will never get there on time,
It's had to stop in the tunnel,
Somewhere down the line.

Some man, rushing to get somewhere,
Couldn't prise himself out of bed;
If he'd allowed more time in the morning,
He wouldn't have lost his head.

The train could have finished its journey,
Passengers on time, after paying their fare;
If he hadn't stuck his head out the window,
Trying to get some fresh air!

UNEXPLAINED DREAM

I had a dream the other night,
That I just can't explain;
I'll try my best to tell you,
Though, to you it may seem tame.

Somebody stopped me in the street,
And asked if I would share,
My comments on certain subjects,
In a questionnaire.

In reality, I wouldn't agree to this,
But in my dream I was a soft touch;
Answering probing questions,
I must have revealed too much.

I vaguely remember the interviewer,
Talking on his mobile phone;
He said he'd got the perfect candidate,
And would meet me at my home.

Before I could get a word in,
Or make any comments either,
He'd got me signed up with a contract,
To be a new bus driver.

I explained I had no reason,
To leave my current work;
I'd been there now for thirty three years,
My boss would go berserk.

Then, as I sat on the top deck of the bus,
He told me my driving style was wrong;
Although he'd never seen me drive,
He said, "This can't go on".

"We can't keep you as a driver,
If you don't change your ways,"
It worried me, and played on my mind,
Throughout the following days.

Then I woke up, quite suddenly,
Even before the alarm;
Realised that I'd been dreaming,
And hadn't come to harm.

I don't answer questions in the street,
And seldom fill in forms sent by post;
It must be thirty years since I last travelled by bus,
A lot less frequent than most.

It's odd, the way your mind plays tricks,
Putting you in preposterous situations;
So real at the time of dreaming,
Everything is an exaggeration.

It's a relief to wake up at the end, though,
And realise that it hasn't been true;
The whole thing has been a peculiar dream,
That came right out of the blue.

MOTORWAY CHAOS

The relentless heat from the noonday sun brought beads of
perspiration to my forehead. It trickled through my hair, and to the
nape of my neck. My shirt, dampened by the moisture, changed colour
round armpits and spine.

Such intensity of the sun's rays were enhanced through the windows
of the stationary vehicle. Too far to walk; too remote to vacate my
seat: too isolated from pedestrian civilisation, and too lethargic, a plan
of escape to even contrive.

Who could have envisaged the traffic chaos that caused this melee of
sweaty bodies to be encaptured behind glass? Certainly not those
attended by the paramedics in the speeding ambulance that passed on
the hard shoulder about twenty minutes ago.

Traffic ahead of us could be seen moving in the distance; pulling to
the right hand side; three lanes merging into one. Several minutes
passed before our coach was thrust into gear, and we inched towards
our destination, speed increasing once past the coned off scene of the
accident, fellow passengers commenting that the driver would be
lucky to survive.

A delay in our journey time is a small price to pay,
The uncomfortable conditions on the upper deck,
No air conditioning working, so we're gasping for breath,
Unlike those pulled from that twisted wreck.

QUESTIONS

Do you ever question things you do?
Do you ever wonder "WHY?"
How do you know what you can achieve,
If you don't give it a try?

Did you ever ask the way to go?
Do you ever question "WHERE?"
How do you know which direction to take,
If there's no one to take you there?

Do you ever question responsibility?
Do you ask the question, "WHO?"
To find out those that can answer,
You'll need information, to accrue.

Did you ever question the time of things?
Do you ever ask, just "WHEN?"
If you never get your timing right,
Will you get the chance to do it again?

Do you ever ponder the method to use?
Do you ever ask the question, "HOW?"
No one is going to chastise you,
You won't get into a row.

Do you ever have to make a choice?
To decide, you need to say, "WHICH?"
To select one, instead of the other,
And to know which one to ditch.

Do you ever wonder about something?
Do you have to ask somebody, "WHAT?"
If no one can tell you the answer to these,
I think you're losing the plot!

THE GALLOWS

The judge put on his small black cap,
"Justice must take its course," he said.
"You'll be taken from this place,
and hung by the neck, until you are dead."

No longer a threat to society,
Ridding the streets of a constant threat;
Allowing women and girls to walk alone,
He deserves all that he gets.

Place a hood on his head; lead him up the steps,
Make him stand on the trap door.
The noose positioned around his neck,
He falls… now he'll kill no more.

Confirmed as dead by the doctors,
A prayer said by a clergyman.
He'll be buried in an unmarked grave,
Taken in a blacked out van.

His family must live in the shadow of guilt,
For his crimes he did certainly pay;
But for people left in the wake of his sins,
They'll not forget him in the cold light of day.

Section 15

GOD CREATES – AND TAKES AWAY

GOD'S CREATION

One day, God was feeling bored,
So he gave his mates his word,
He said, "With you I'll make a little bet.
I'll design, if I can,
What will be known as Man,
It'll be the best design that I've done yet."

"Man will need a heart that beats,
A stomach and mouth so he can eat,
I think I'll call him Adam, from this day.
He'll have legs so he can walk,
And a tongue so he can talk,
And a mind to make him choose which part he'll play."

"I'll give him feet so he can run,
I'd better make a hole in his bum,
He'll need to rid his body of its waste.
Now, let me stop and think,
He'll need a way to drink,
I'll combine his mouth and tongue to give him taste."

"He'll have eight fingers and two thumbs,
And teeth growing from his gums,
To help him eat the food that he'll require.
I'll put hands on each of his arms,
Give him a temper he'll need to keep calm,
Pores in his skin, so his body can perspire."

"Finally, my aim,
Is to give Adam a brain,
So he can make decisions in his life.
Unfortunately, with this,
The one thing that I've missed,
The poor bloke's going to need a lady wife."

"I think that I will win my bet,
If I can aim to get,
The whole job done in less than seven days.
Next week I'll start on Eve,
Who'll need a way to conceive,
So I'll modify her design in subtle ways."

"She'll need amending from the start,
So that their body parts,
Can connect when they are feeling really close.
She'll need a womb to grow their young,
After Adam's had his fun,
And her belly then will swell bigger than most."

"I'll do this project on my own,
Adam will be all home grown,
So any faults will be down to me.
They can talk to me in church,
I won't leave them in the lurch,
They'd better consider starting a Family Tree."

"They will settle on the Earth,
And as they will be first,
I'd like to think they'd live their lives entwined.
So, now I'll sit back in the sun,
And observe what I have done,
As the pair of them start to procreate Mankind."

" Well, my job is nearly done,
And the bet is surely won,
My creation will be very hard to better.
So, to the future generations,
That will spread through many nations,
I've done my work, now follow it to the letter."

"You'll never be on your own,
But when your young are grown,
I'd like you to instruct them, wrong from right.
I've done my very best,
Now I'm putting you to the test,
I'll be watching you, although I'm out of sight."

"Any decisions that you make,
Any wrong turns that you take,
Any problems that seem to come out of the blue;
Never worry, never fear,
For I'll always be here,
I will always, and forever, watch over you."

A SMASHING PARTY

It'd been a smashing party,
The best they'd attended by far;
They waved goodbye to the other guests,
As all six crammed into the car.

The driver hadn't had much to drink,
Well, that's what he told his mates;
As he reversed out of the parking space,
And drove out of the gates.

It was two o'clock in the early hours,
They sang to the radio's refrain;
Not long now before they're home,
As they sped down the country lane.

As they rounded a corner,
They saw an obstacle, partly concealed;
He slammed his foot on the brake pedal,
The car skidded, and flew into a field.

The fence acted as a barrier,
To keep in the farmer's horses;
But the momentum of the speeding car,
Meant that it somersaulted.

It gouged into the muddy field,
It was night, so they couldn't see,
The outline of what lay ahead,
As the car wrapped itself round a tree.

The front of the vehicle was crunched up small,
Pinning the driver into his seat;
The steering wheel penetrated his torso,
While the engine trapped his feet.

There was no movement from him or his mates,
No groans, or signs of life.
Only the hissing of the steam,
From the radiator in the night.

The lights of the car had all gone out,
With the impact, and this sorry state;
No one would spot the car on this road,
The hour was very late.

As dawn approached, the car was seen
By a driver of a passing van;
He called the police and ambulance
Saying, "Get here as fast as you can".

They pulled six bodies from the wreck,
Their families must be told;
It's not a nice job, but it must be done,
None of them were very old.

Six lives wiped out in an instant;
Six families with one member less;
The police would break the news gently,
Then clean up the bloody mess.

Oh, what a party it must have been,
The best one ever, I think;
But was any of it worth it?
Could it be blamed on the drink?

No more parties for those in the car,
No more invitations to send;
They had their party, and paid the price,
Now they've met an untimely end.

BY CHOICE

His dark trousers hung loosely beyond his shoes,
Tattered and frayed, where they dragged on the ground.
They were tied with string around his waist,
The shoes were odd ones he'd found.

His coat was stained, and ripped in parts,
No buttons to hold it together.
He huddled inside its vast extent,
To protect him from the weather.

He shuffled along the busy street,
Checking bins for what he could find.
Anything of use, or to eat, would do,
He didn't really mind.

His pockets bulged with what he'd picked up.
He smoked a butt he'd plucked from the floor.
Whiskers adorned his weathered face,
And his feet were blistered and sore.

He'd had a family, and home of his own,
But his world had fallen apart.
When his job was lost, and then his wife,
He decided to make a new start.

He looked down and out to the people he passed,
They all agreed that, with one voice.
But he was happy in his own little world,
Because he lived this way by choice.

DEATH BECKONS

From the moment that we enter this world,
(And, this fact, there's no denying),
Though we hope to stay for many years,
Every one of us is dying!

We may survive for a hundred years,
Or go in our sleep tomorrow;
But the time allocated is all you've got,
There's no more that you can borrow.

No, we're all on a downward spiral,
From the moment we draw our first breath;
So, why worry about what goes on in life,
Because we're not that far away from death!

JUST ONE MORE...

The stomach clenches, and the mouth runs dry,
At the sight of the upturned bottle, behind the bar.
One drink is too many...Twenty, not enough,
You know you've already had too much, by far.

But the bottle is there, beckoning you,
Tempting you, with its intoxicating charm.
You're fighting to control that rising urge,
One more drink would do no harm.

You check your wallet; there's not much left,
But you can still have just one more.
"One for the road", as the saying goes,
As you stumble and hit the floor.

A disembodied voice, in the distance, somewhere,
Say's, "Get him out of here...He's had enough,"
But you only see legs and feet, all blurred,
Thanks to that bottle of amber stuff.

A drink at home will do the trick,
It'll make you feel better, so you say.
But the appeal of the bottle has grabbed you,
And controls your life, night and day.

If you want to be sick in the gutter,
And talk with a slur to your voice,
To pee your trousers, in public,
Don't blame the bottle – it's your choice!

GOOD GOD!

As God reaches down to take your hand,
He'll lead you to that promised land.

He'll introduce you to all of his mates,
As St. Peter opens those Pearly Gates.

You'll be allocated your personal cloud,
And a set of wings to make you proud.

When you drift above us all,
Remember when you got that call.

Your time on Earth had made you ill,
Life had been a bitter pill.

But now there's peace within your heart,
It stopped beating on Earth, yet in Heaven restarts.

Now you can reach to the ones you love,
As your cloud floats by, high above.

If you can get a message into their minds,
They can talk to you at any time.

Just because your life has been curtailed,
Doesn't mean there's nothing beyond your cloud.

Keep in touch with those left behind,
They'll be timid at first, I think you'll find.

It's hard to convince that someone's still there,
When they've been buried in a graveyard somewhere.

But now you've reached that sacred place,
And met God in person, face to face.

You're in the best spot to tell the rest,
That where you are now is certainly best.

Don't worry about you... no tears, no frown,
For you will always be looking down.

FROM TRUST, TO LUST

A child from a troubled background,
Or an unstable family life,
Can't cope with their fragile surroundings,
And need freeing from their strife.

The Welfare State takes them into care,
And places them into a foster home.
Where they can be integrated into a family unit,
Whose affection and concern is shown.

Sometimes, in a few isolated cases,
And often, after several years have gone by,
The child can reveal a dark secret,
Of the time when the love did die.

A lapsed moment when they were off guard,
What was a friendly night time cuddle,
Turned into a hand upon the leg,
And the confused child's mind was in a muddle.

As the time went by, the touches got worse,
And the frequency increased.
He said, "It's our secret… so don't say a word,"
The attention just never ceased.

As a child, with nowhere to turn for help,
When the one you live with is your foe,
You can't talk about your problem,
There is nowhere for you to go.

The touches turn to stroking of the hair,
And the soothing talk gets more intimate.
Familiarity grows as the abuse takes a hold,
And the perpetrator gets more confident.

The child is scared of the person in charge,
The one who cuddles and caresses their body.
They can't be brushed off, or even ignored,
For their action is extremely shoddy.

Who will believe what the child has to say?
Who can they go and tell?
The longer it lasts, the harder it gets,
When they know that all is not well.

The pervert who touches the little kids,
Should be locked up, and the key thrown away.
They should be removed from roaming the streets,
And be imprisoned, for life and a day.

The child's life started off on the wrong foot,
And instead of getting better, got worse.
They didn't deserve what they've had to face,
Their guardian, becoming a curse.

The mind of the child can be damaged for years,
And their future relationships marred,
And all because, the one they should trust,
Had left them brutally scarred.

TRAGEDY

The family group huddled together,
Not conscious of the rain;
Consoling arms around their shoulders,
Unable to ease the pain.

They stood at the roadside on the grass,
Next to a sycamore tree;
Skid marks crossed the tarmac surface,
There for all to see.

Blue and white remnants fluttered,
In the breeze of the early daybreak;
Shards of glass and plastic littered
Where the police had their barrier of tape.

Traffic still passed on the busy road,
Oblivious to all that had occurred;
But the family stood there… staring,
Praying, not saying a word.

The police had told them, at their house,
Of an accident in the dark;
Now they stood, and stared at that fatal tree,
Gouges scored into its bark.

Silently reliving their memories,
Of a member of their clan,
A mothers loss; a brother gone;
He'll never get to be a man.

Only recently he'd got his beloved car,
For passing his exams; it was a treat,
Not for long did he live to use his skills,
He should have strapped himself into his seat.

A small, furry teddy was tied to the tree,
A bunch of flowers laid on the ground;
The scuff in the grass where his car had ploughed,
Had formed a muddy mound.

Tears filled the eyes of onlookers,
As the family hid their grief;
Not talking, but inwardly praying
To God, who was their belief.

Stepping away from this tragic death site,
Now a roadside memorial;
A reminder for other road users,
A warning, visible to all.

Safety signs along the roadside,
An ironic situation to have to face;
Where the long, straight stretch of tarmac,
Was an ideal place to race.

Who knows what happened that dreadful night,
Nobody was there to see;
He'd always been warned about taking care,
But said, "It'll never happen to me."

In those early hours, we know it DID happen,
And although they don't know the facts,
It won't replace the boy that's now missing,
In the family, it's left a big gap.

So a message from the heart to all drivers,
Who think speed is all they should know;
It could be you that lies next in the morgue,
So, Please, Please, Please… go slow!!!

WELL... DO YOU?

Paedophiles are now quite common place,
In every news bulletin, there's a few.
With stories about child abduction,
Do you want one living next door to you?

The innocence of children has been taken,
Their freedom has been snatched away.
Unable to play, unsupervised,
Anywhere, anytime, anyday.

When I was a boy, we spent our time
Playing in the open air.
We'd ride our bikes for miles, and miles,
And nobody seemed to care.

You never heard of children being grabbed,
And disappearing from sight.
There was never any threat of anyone
Molesting kiddies, day or night.

With the introduction of computer systems,
And since the internet was born,
There's an increase in the number of people,
Logging on to view child porn.

There's a call for the names of convicted men,
Who've served their time, and been released,
To be made public, so every parent,
Can protect their children from the beast.

The child shouldn't become a lure for his lust,
A potential victim falling foul to his prey.
They should be guarded, with the full force of the law,
To keep the threat at bay.

CHEERS! ...DON'T GET SMASHED

How many people must die each year
As you climb in your car... slip it into gear;
You'd been in the pub, a few drinks with friends,
Sober enough to negotiate the road and its bends.

Another statistic for this Christmas season,
Another mortuary slab occupied for no reason;
There's others on the road, besides you,
Several have celebrated with a drink or two.

You may think you can drive, but in reality
You'll probably end up as another fatality;
So forget that drink that's offered to you,
It's illegal to drive when you've had a few.

You may survive a serious accident,
And your car may not have much more than a dent;
It's not like in films when they say, "Bang – you're dead,"
Your brain could get mangled inside your head.

Mutilation and scars, that will last through your days,
A cripple, relying on help in every way;
Unable to walk, confined to a chair,
Your mind like a vegetable, needing constant care.

What kind of life is that for the sake of a drink?
Just take a second to stop and think;
Leave your car at home, and then without fear,
You'll enjoy your Christmas, and see the New Year.

LUCKY ESCAPE

He sat in his car,
Near where kids play.
He'd been watching one,
Best part of the day.

He grabbed the girl
Roughly by the arm.
He said, "Be quiet,
And I'll do you no harm."

Into the car he pushed her,
With quite some force.
She had tears in her eyes,
But he showed no remorse.

She screamed and struggled,
As she tried to get out.
But with the windows closed,
Nobody heard her shouts.

He drove the car
Into a field,
Then wrestled with her,
Trying to make her yield.

Her screams were heard,
As she kicked and fought.
That's what the class
At school had been taught.

"Make as much noise
As you can,
To get away from
That despicable man".

He failed to hold her,
She was like an eel.
As she wriggled and squirmed,
It made her feel ill.

His grip relaxed
On her little arm,
As she turned and fled,
Spared from his harm.

He didn't chase,
But let her run.
As she headed home,
And to her mum.

The police were informed
Of the incident.
Of the man who'd pounced
With malicious intent.

They couldn't trace him,
With the information shared,
But the worrying fact is
He's still out there somewhere.

UNHEALTHY SITUATION

The place? A detached bungalow,
The people? They were quite nice;
Inside, everything was chaos,
A breeding ground for mice.

Mother and daughter lived in the property,
The man of the house was not well;
Suffering from long term illness,
From the house emanated a smell.

It hit you, as you entered the door,
It didn't take long to decipher why;
For all around were piles of clothes,
And dirty dishes stacked up high.

The table was littered with papers,
Empty drink cans not thrown away;
Takeaways half eaten in containers,
Left by the women, over several days.

Casual tables, with too much junk accumulated,
So full, they couldn't take any more;
The surplus, already toppled from the mound,
Lay scattered over the floor.

The kitchen sink wasn't visible,
Beneath dirty dishes, plates and cups;
Not rinsed, or washed, or put away,
Left festering, the filth building up.

Dirty washing on the floor,
No room on any work surface;
The pile never diminishing in its size,
The washer, seemingly serving no purpose.

Clothes that had supposedly been washed,
Formed a mound by the back door.
Not ironed, or even folded,
All creased, just left on the floor.

Two cats live amongst this chaos,
In the kitchen, their litter tray;
Mess, growing white with age and fungus,
Accumulated over many a day.

The women just sit there, watching TV,
Mainly cartoons, all day long;
Very often, not even getting dressed,
Oblivious to the stagnant pong.

For the sake of the man, who's unable to help,
I reckon it would take two days, at best;
Of continuously digging into the task,
To tidy up all of the mess.

His health, surely, cannot benefit,
From the mayhem in which he's placed;
Nor the carers who have to tend him,
And the conditions with which they're faced.

The spare bedroom should first be cleared of junk,
And with only minor alteration,
Could be fitted with simple shelving,
To take all of his medication.

That would free up a lot of room,
In other bedrooms, and the hall;
Making room to manoeuvre his wheelchair,
Giving space, so no one would fall.

The room now available in the bedrooms,
Once tidied, would be quite vast;
They'd need to fill loads of rubbish sacks,
Uncovering the floor, at last.

Once the rubbish had been thrown out,
Then the clean clothes could be stored away;
Each in their own environment,
In a place, where they should stay.

I think, without exaggeration,
A skip could be filled quite well;
Just by throwing out things not needed,
And black sacks of crap, they cannot sell.

A major overhaul is needed,
Because the place is simply a tip;
The women need to get off of their arses,
And tidy up a bit.

At least throw away food containers,
And wash their dishes in the sink;
But all they do, is sit there,
They don't even seem to think.

It could be a really nice bungalow,
If everything was put in its place;
For now, it's absolutely disgusting,
But something, unfortunately, carers must face.

OUT OF SERVICE

No daylight had penetrated the confines of the room,
For a considerable length of time;
The oak door, with its iron latch and studs,
Was scarred with years of grime.

It creaked, where it's hinges lacked lubricant,
High-pitched screeches filled the air;
Echoing through the empty structure,
That for years, had been stripped bare.

Dust and cobwebs, festooned the space,
In that isolated cell;
The air was damp, and the atmosphere,
Was filled with a putrid smell.

A fluttering in the corner,
Made our heart rates pound;
Feathers, and birds faeces,
Were spread across the ground.

As our eyes adjusted to the dark,
We could distinguish through the gloom,
Ropes, looped from the ceiling,
Of that darkened room.

The church hadn't been used for many years,
When the toll of the bells ceased to sound;
In this room, the ropes would be pulled and tugged,
By folk trying to keep feet on the ground.

The massive bells were long since removed,
Now the emptiness made us feel nervous;
As our voices echoed round those sacred walls,
That will never again ring out during a religious service.